The Professional Agile Leader

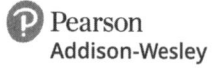

The Professional Agile Leader

THE LEADER'S JOURNEY TOWARD GROWING MATURE AGILE TEAMS AND ORGANIZATIONS

Ron Eringa
Kurt Bittner
Laurens Bonnema

✦✦ Addison-Wesley

Boston • Columbus • New York • San Francisco • Amsterdam • Cape Town
Dubai • London • Madrid • Milan • Munich • Paris • Montreal • Toronto • Delhi • Mexico City
São Paulo • Sydney • Hong Kong • Seoul • Singapore • Taipei • Tokyo

Pearson's Commitment to Diversity, Equity, and Inclusion

Pearson is dedicated to creating bias-free content that reflects the diversity of all learners. We embrace the many dimensions of diversity, including but not limited to race, ethnicity, gender, socioeconomic status, ability, age, sexual orientation, and religious or political beliefs.

Education is a powerful force for equity and change in our world. It has the potential to deliver opportunities that improve lives and enable economic mobility. As we work with authors to create content for every product and service, we acknowledge our responsibility to demonstrate inclusivity and incorporate diverse scholarship so that everyone can achieve their potential through learning. As the world's leading learning company, we have a duty to help drive change and live up to our purpose to help more people create a better life for themselves and to create a better world.

Our ambition is to purposefully contribute to a world where:

- Everyone has an equitable and lifelong opportunity to succeed through learning.
- Our educational products and services are inclusive and represent the rich diversity of learners.
- Our educational content accurately reflects the histories and experiences of the learners we serve.
- Our educational content prompts deeper discussions with learners and motivates them to expand their own learning (and worldview).

While we work hard to present unbiased content, we want to hear from you about any concerns or needs with this Pearson product so that we can investigate and address them.

- Please contact us with concerns about any potential bias at https://www.pearson.com/report-bias.html.

CONTENTS

FOREWORD

I recently was talking to an executive about their agile transition. He described a series of great successes and disappointing failures. As we talked about these situations, picking at the "why?", the "what", and the "how could we have done better?" I was struck by a single truth: The failures were never about the Scrum Team or Teams; the failures were always about the friction created by agile teams within an existing, industrial-minded organization. And many of these failures were ultimately about leadership and the missteps they made as they tried to navigate the disconnect between these two paradigms.

One story, in particular, stood out to me. The story was about a Sprint Review that did not go well. The Sprint Goal was poorly formed, the team did not really understand what they were trying to deliver on, and the most important stakeholders and management were invited and actually showed up. The Sprint Review did what it was meant to do: It exposed the challenges the team faced and highlighted their misunderstanding, but it also showed how lacking the whole organization was in support of the ultimate Product Goal. It was not a fun or pleasant event. And everyone not only felt upset afterward but also questioned their contribution and work during the Sprint.

What happened next, however, was worse. The senior leader involved came after the Scrum Team both as a group and individually. He told them that "he never wanted to be embarrassed like that again," and that "many of them need to think about their career choices." He asked for them not to engage with senior stakeholders and to allow him to manage all interactions with those stakeholders. In that one response, he not only destroyed any motivation the Scrum Team had but also their desire to use an empirical process, to be agile.

You can guess what happened in the next Sprint Review. Everything was "great," no senior stakeholders were invited, and it really was just a progress report for the senior leader who was present. The project slowly disappeared as the Scrum Team members found other projects that were more important.

This example is extreme, but in many subtle ways, this happens frequently as the leadership in an organization tries to protect their image, or ensure that everything is working the way they want. And it makes sense. Traditional approaches encourage structured communication channels and the importance of political capital. They encourage everything green or amber on your executive dashboard. It is easy to see what that senior leader did wrong when talking about that particular Sprint Review, but how does an agile leader do things right? What does it take to be an agile leader?

When I talk to managers and executives at large organizations, I am often asked, "The Scrum Guide has no role for me. What do I do now?" This one question is actually two questions. The first question is, what is the practical reality of the impact of Scrum on their situation. What happens to their existing responsibilities and accountabilities, and what does that mean for the Scrum Team and the problem they are solving. The second question is much deeper. What is the role of leadership, and what is leadership in the postindustrial world?

This book actually provides materials for both questions. By drawing on their vast experience, Ron, Kurt, and Laurens have described the reality of many situations, teasing out the practical tips and patterns for good leadership.

They provide guidance on how a leader can help shape the environment for agile teams to succeed. They cover some hard topics, including the importance of purpose and mission, how to change to an outcome-focused rather than output-focused organization, the power of servant leadership, and even the thorny topic of the value of leadership. Many of the lessons they describe resonate with me from my own experience and what I observe in others. The narrative style of the book makes it easy to read, and I am sure that there will be many times that you see yourself in Doreen and the friction that is created between the agile and traditional approaches to value.

Ron, Kurt, and Laurens have written a book that tells a story about how traditional, industrial organizations need to change to take advantage of and survive the digital age. They focus on leaders and the harsh reality that many of the truths that traditional management encourages need to be rethought when change is the norm, opportunity is everywhere, and disaster is just around the corner.

I hope you enjoy reading this book as much as I did and that you take a few things with you as you try and change the world and thrive in that change.

—*Dave West*
CEO, Scrum.org

PREFACE

The bookshelves of the world abound with books on leadership. Authors of diverse backgrounds serve up a steady stream of titles that inspire admiration and imitation of the examples set by great leaders. And yet, despite all this, many still strain against the yoke of bad leaders, toiling pointlessly toward uncertain goals and wondering, "When will things be different?"

We think there are two problems with most literature on leadership. First, focusing on the behavior of great leaders gives little insight into how leadership develops. We rarely see their uncertain early steps, the difficult choices and circumstances that led them to make different choices, or the price they paid for choosing a different way. We see the leader-hero in their maturity, haloed in myth, but never as the stumbling student or the uncertain professional taking their first steps toward the person they later become.

The other problem with the cult of the leader-hero is that it overshadows the daily acts of leadership that make progress possible. Leaders are not superheroes. Leaders, in our view, are everywhere. Or, rather, opportunities for leadership are everywhere, waiting to be seized.

We don't think that leaders are born with some special qualities that make them great leaders. The great leaders with whom we have worked are regular people who care deeply about helping others to achieve shared goals, and who have had the good fortune to have had experiences that have shown them a different way to lead people. We believe that leadership is a learned response to challenges in the world, and that everyone can lead at different points. To meet the challenges in our complex world, we, in fact, need everyone to lead at different times.

This book is about how people learn to embrace their leadership potential, how they let go of their preconceptions about what leaders do, and how they learn from each other how to work together to reach a better future. Our goal is to share what we have learned about what leaders do, how they think, and, most importantly, how they got there. We hope it helps you in your own leadership journey.

—Ron, Kurt, and Laurens
April 2022

INTRODUCTION

"Do not follow in the footsteps of the wise.
Seek what they sought."

—Matsuo Basho (1644–1694)

The world over, even the most successful organizations are scrambling to keep pace with unrelenting change. No matter their past success, their future isn't guaranteed the way it once was. Past success, in fact, tends to make people complacent at a time they most need to change. As customers and competitors respond to change, markets shift, tastes change, and dominant market positions can disappear overnight.

The phrase we most often hear from executives is that they want their organizations to be more agile. Nimble. Responsive. Because the disruptions they feel are most often in the digital parts of their business, they often turn to agile development frameworks like Scrum for inspiration in their change. These frameworks certainly help development teams achieve agility. And yet, the executives say that either they can't scale the change beyond a few teams or the change doesn't seem to stick. Something is missing.

Agility, or as we prefer to call it, responsiveness, results from deep changes to the culture of the organization. *Culture* is a simple word for a subtle and complex combination of norms, values, and situational responses. Changing culture is not easy, nor should it be, for it acts like a force that binds together the people in a society, a group, and even an organization.

Leaders transmit the culture within their organizations—not in explicit ways, and not by dictum or directive, but rather by demonstration: By modeling appropriate and desired behaviors, they shape the culture that, in turn, guides their organizations. So, to help their organizations become more responsive, the leaders in the organization need to change.

PURPOSE OF THIS BOOK

Leaders have a tough challenge: While they strive to create greater team engagement and ownership, their organization's culture usually rewards compliance and fault-prevention instead of creativity, self-organization, and autonomy. And they live in an unforgiving spotlight and cannot rely on trial and error, our natural means of learning new things. Lacking mentors who can show them the way, they have few places to turn.

Our goal is to describe the journey of typical leaders in an organization as they face the challenge of changing their own organization while also changing themselves. The journeys they take are far from perfect; expect them to experiment, make mistakes, learn, and to adapt. While the journey in this book is fictionalized, the stories are all based on real situations the authors have either lived or witnessed. And while the stories don't deal with every possible situation you might encounter, they include the most common ones that nearly every leader faces.

Every agile leader's journey is different; each takes a different path, and each faces different challenges. Yet each shares a singular goal: to help their organization achieve resilience and flexibility while seeking success in a changing and challenging world. In this book, we share, in various forms, our own experiences on our own journeys. While we can't claim to be the wise people to whom Basho referred, by sharing our experiences, we hope to give you ideas, approaches, and techniques that will help you on your own journey. But you will have to find your own way, and find what works for you and your organization.

By the end of this book, we hope that you will take a different approach to the leadership challenges that you face. While we can't tell you what to do, the scenarios described in the book will help you to find your own way to help your organization to adapt and improve.

WHO SHOULD READ THIS BOOK

This book provides leaders, at any level, with or without formal authority, with strategies and mental models that will help them to support and grow agile teams in their organization. Managers of teams and managers of functional areas that support teams will find strategies for overcoming the challenges they face and the journeys they need to travel to achieve their full potential as leaders. Senior executives will gain a greater understanding of the challenges their managers face in changing not only the way they work, but also the way they regard their role in the organization. Finally, Scrum Masters, Product Owners, and team members will gain a greater appreciation of the challenges that managers in their organization face, and how they also need to exhibit leadership to help their managers, teams, and organization grow.

HOW THIS BOOK IS ORGANIZED

This book follows the journey of a CEO who is leading the acquisition of a fast-growing company as she seeks to learn how her own company can become equally successful. Readers will watch the struggles that this leader works through as she also works to change herself and the organization around her. The story is a fictionalized amalgamation of the authors' own experiences and those of our clients and peers; any resemblance to actual people or specific events is accidental.

The story describes typical challenges that leaders confront when they help their organizations shift toward agility. As in many of the real-life situations, you will discover quite late in the story that real agility requires a shift in culture (Chapters 5 and 8). After reading this book, you will be ready to start your agile leadership journey by applying the lessons from these late chapters. In this way, you can avoid many of the pitfalls and frustrations in Doreen's story and be a better leader to your agile teams.

Although the authors are all deeply engaged with the Scrum community, this book does not require knowledge of Scrum. We have deliberately avoided using Scrum-specific terms, events, and roles, and have opted for more general descriptions to emphasize that the approach described in the book can be used with any agile approach.

The main action takes place in an old, large-scale, traditional energy company. The narrative journey of the organization is interspersed with commentary and reflection on the challenges most organizations face, and discussion of strategies they can take to meet those challenges head-on. The intention is not to provide a complete narrative for the examples shown; rather, the vignettes simply illustrate critical events in the journey of the agile leader.

At the end of each chapter is a sketchnoted visual summary (by Laurens) showing the chapter's key lessons, from the perspective of Doreen, the protagonist agile leader. These visualizations aim to remind and reinforce the concepts presented in the chapter using a fresh style. These sketchnotes are collected in Appendix B.

Chapter 1: An Organization at a Crossroads describes a once-successful organization that has lost its way. It can no longer survive by depending on its traditional business model, and it is struggling to be more responsive to customers and competitors. Infighting and frustration are limiting the organization's ability to respond, and the steps it has taken toward agility have been largely ineffective. The CEO is in charge of acquiring a company with the intention of adapting its strategy to get back in the game. The way forward is not clear.

Chapter 2: Forming Teams and Discovering Purpose describes how empowering cross-functional teams is the starting point for agile change. Finding the right people, with the right skills, attitudes, and motivations, is an essential but often overlooked starting point. Once formed, these teams first have to rediscover why they exist and what they are trying to achieve. As most organizations discover when they try to do this, it's harder than they expected. Everyone thinks they know what customers want and who their real customers are, yet the scant data they have does not support this. They quickly realize they need better data, fresher insights, and faster feedback.

Chapter 3: Shifting from Output to Impact describes how the teams and their leaders struggle to shift their focus from performing work to achieving results. Measuring work was easy; they just watched what people did and compared it to the plan. But now they realize that measuring to the plan told them nothing about the impact their work had on customers and on business success. As they improve their delivery frequency, they start to realize how far off the mark their plans really were, and they are filled with both despair and hope. It's an important turning point for everyone.

Chapter 4: Learning to Let Go describes how the teams and their leaders are changing by becoming more feedback-driven. To act more rapidly on that feedback, the teams take on more responsibility for making their own decisions, but that doesn't sit well with some of the former managers, who feel their authority and status are being undermined. Even some team members struggle with where they fit into the organization and how to move ahead. Those who overcome this discomfort find new ways of contributing and new sources of satisfaction.

Chapter 5: The Predictable Existential Crisis describes what happens when nascent agile teams, experiencing successes but also still struggling with their own issues, feel growing pressure from the parent organization over the changes they are making. Managers in other parts of the parent organization feel threatened by the results the teams are achieving, and they are putting pressure on the CEO to make the agile organization "play by the rules." But the CEO likes the progress she is seeing and wants to understand more about what the agile teams are doing that is different.

Chapter 6: Leaders, Everywhere describes how team members also learn how to lead, and why cultivating leadership at all levels helps the organization to become more responsive and resilient. Leadership is an activity, not a role, and the mission of leaders is to help other leaders to grow. As the organization learns how to embrace self-organization, growing leadership at all levels is a key enabler.

Chapter 7: Aligning the Organization describes how, as organizations grow their agility, team by team, product by product, they come to a point where they must either fully commit to continuing their agile journey or they will fall back to the old ways of working. Organizations can continue for a long time with two different operating models, one agile and one traditional, coexisting side-by-side. But they cannot maintain these two models forever; eventually they have to choose. This chapter is about how they make those choices to prevent themselves from sliding back to old ways of working.

Chapter 8: Aligning the Culture describes how the final, and most impactful, challenge the agile leader faces is changing the culture of the organization. Culture encompasses the social behavior and norms that people in the organization exhibit, including their beliefs and habits. In changing the organization's culture to embrace and embody agility, the agile leader ensures that agility will survive and thrive in the face of future disruptions.

Appendix A: Patterns and Anti-Patterns for Effective Leadership describes traditional leadership behaviors that are less effective in helping teams to develop effective self-managing behaviors, alongside behaviors that agile leaders can adopt to help their teams develop effective self-managing behaviors.

This provides a quick reference to which agile leaders can refer to help to catch themselves from falling back into old habits.

Appendix B: Doreen's Sketchnotes collects the sketchnote summaries presented at the end of each chapter to provide a quick visual reference for the book as a whole.

Our intent is to take you on the typical journey that agile leaders take, to help you to experience, vicariously, the leadership transformation that we, our clients, and our peers have gone through. Our hope is that as you read these experiences and our reflections upon them, you will find the stories and commentary useful in helping you on your own agile journey.

To help you begin planning your own leadership journey, the last chapter contains a few concrete guidelines. These guidelines will help you get started and better prepare you to learn from the mistakes we made. But don't skip ahead; these recommendations will be more meaningful in the context of the journey described in the preceding chapters.

Without further ado, it's time to begin where nearly all agile journeys begin, with an organization struggling to reinvent itself in a changing world.

Register your copy of *The Professional Agile Leader* on the InformIT site for convenient access to updates and/or corrections as they become available. To start the registration process, go to informit.com/register and log in or create an account. Enter the product ISBN (9780137591510) and click Submit. Look on the Registered Products tab for an Access Bonus Content link next to this product, and follow that link to access any available bonus materials. If you would like to be notified of exclusive offers on new editions and updates, please check the box to receive email from us.

ACKNOWLEDGMENTS

Behind the authors of every book stands a community of people who helped refine the ideas, improve the expression of those ideas, or simply carve out time to craft the expression of those ideas. This book would not exist without the support and encouragement of many people.

Our colleagues in the Scrum.org community, including Ken Schwaber, whose commitment to empiricism and bottom-up intelligence continue to challenge us to look at leadership challenges with fresh eyes; Dave West, whose support and encouragement enabled us to carve out time to work on the book; Patricia Kong, who serves as an example of how empowering a community can bring people together to achieve more than they could as individuals; and Ryan Ripley and John Davis, who helped us to shape the leadership stories in our Professional Agile Leadership training, well before this book was conceived.

Our colleagues in our extended leadership community, notably Steven Happee and Jorgen Hesselberg, whose keen eyes and thoughtful intellects challenged us to better express ourselves; and Rini van Solingen, who provided feedback on our first rough book ideas and shared his experiences in writing.

Our myriad clients, colleagues, and trainees over the many years of our careers, who have shaped our views on leadership and whose experiences inspired us to craft the storyline in this book.

Our colleagues at Pearson, including Haze Humbert and the team of editors and production professionals, who helped turn our ideas into a published volume.

And finally, our families, who graciously and patiently gave us the time for writing, rewriting and sketching the work you read here.

ABOUT THE AUTHORS

Ron Eringa is a Leadership Developer. His mission is to create organizations where people love to work and where real customer value is created. In the last 20 years, he has built expertise on how to lead IT organizations that use agile and Scrum. After an initial education in electrical engineering and software engineering, Ron ended up in different leadership roles. In these roles he discovered the leadership capabilities that are essential to create autonomous teams with a high level of maturity and creativity. He believes that autonomous teams are the fundamental core of a modern organization that thrives in this complex and ever-changing world. Many of the stories in this book were shaped while Ron was developing the Professional Agile Leadership class together with leadership experts in the Scrum.org community. By mixing in his expertise on cultural change and leadership development, Ron hopes to inspire a large audience of leaders to reach their full potential.

Kurt Bittner has been delivering working products in short, feedback-driven cycles for nearly 40 years and has helped many organizations do the same. He is particularly interested in helping people form strong, self-organizing, high-performance teams that deliver solutions that customers love, and helping organizations use empirical feedback to achieve customer outcome-focused goals. He is an author or editor of many books on agile product development, including *Mastering Professional Scrum*, *The Zombie Scrum Survival Guide*, *The Nexus Framework for Scaling Scrum*, *The Professional Scrum Team*, and *Professional Agile Leadership*, as well as *The Guide to Evidence-Based Management* and *The Nexus Guide*.

Laurens Bonnema is an Agile Trainer and Management Consultant and a mentor to leaders creating resilient organizations at any scale. He has a strong background in IT, with experience in almost every role. As a Professional Scrum Master, Certified Scrum Master, Certified Scrum Product Owner, Certified Agile Master, Agile Master Assessor, IPMA Agile Assessor, and PRINCE2 Practitioner, Laurens strives to merge classic and agile management in the conviction that it is the future of professional management. As a Professional Scrum Trainer and SAFe Program Consultant, he helps to improve the profession of software delivery as well as marketing, human resources, and finance. Laurens brings to his teaching his experience in enterprise IT since 1999 and on Scrum Teams since 2006. He is a driving force in the Agile community and a sought-after speaker at conferences and events.

AN ORGANIZATION AT A CROSSROADS

Organizations riding high on waves of success don't feel the need to change. All too often, they remain comfortably complacent even as their positions slowly erode. Only when their existing management approaches and business models are imminently threatened do they start to feel that, perhaps, they should try something different. By then, it can be too late.

Even foresighted leaders who see the challenges ahead may have trouble motivating their organizations to change. People get comfortable with their existing way of working, and while they welcome incremental improvements to the status quo, motivating sweeping change is all but impossible. And agile change, by its very nature, is sweeping, disruptive change.

Leaders who want to help their organizations adapt to increasing competition and uncertainties need to find pockets in their organization that need to work in a different way to succeed, and then help these parts of their organization find their own way of working. No leader will be able to overcome the inertia of the larger organization's complacency overnight, but by focusing on smaller pockets of innovation, such a leader can slowly start to shift the balance in favor of the necessary broader changes.

COMPLEX CHALLENGES CREATE URGENCY FOR AGILITY

Doreen is the CEO for a traditional electrical utility, Reliable Energy, with a history going back more than 100 years. Its current business model is based on supplying energy from its own generation facilities over its own grid, which is in turn connected to regional and national grids that allow the firm to sell and buy power from other similar companies. This business model is being challenged by new independent distributed generation technologies like wind, solar, and other technologies that provide energy more cheaply and more sustainably. Reliable Energy has begun to accept that its government-granted monopoly will eventually be withdrawn, and it needs to develop new products and services, and new business models, if it is to survive and thrive in the future.

"Welcome, everyone. Thank you for making time in your busy schedules to let me share some exciting news. Effective today, we have acquired a fast-growing company called Energy Bridge to accelerate our transition from being a traditional energy producer to a manager of smart grids that connect distributed energy producers with energy consumers. Energy Bridge will be managed as an independent subsidiary, with its CEO, Nagesh, reporting directly to me.

"As many of you know, there is a competition under way for a multi-country smart grid management system, with tenders due at the end of the year. It is important for our future that we win this contract as the foundation for our future business model. Nagesh, could you share our vision for how Energy Bridge helps us to build a new business model?"

"Thanks, Doreen. As some of you may already know, Energy Bridge has developed and marketed a smart home controller that manages energy production, storage, and interface with the grid. It balances supply and demand, and takes advantage of smart bidirectional charging of electric vehicles (EVs) to store electricity close to where it is generated, by using the EV or other battery storage to power the home, and it sells energy to the grid when rates are attractive. Our experience in delivering this product to customers has given us insights that will help us create new grid management services that can drive the new business model for Reliable Energy in the future."

"Thanks, Nagesh. As Nagesh has suggested, this acquisition gives us a platform on which we can build our future strategy, and a customer base from which we can learn. To help us learn quickly, Nagesh has agreed to lead our Smart Grid initiative in addition to leading the Energy Bridge business unit. And with that, I am sure you have questions. Keep in mind that this is just the first of regular updates we will hold over the coming months, so if we don't have time to get to your questions today, send them to me or Nagesh and we will make sure we get to them on future calls."

Later, as Nagesh and Doreen are leaving the meeting, Nagesh comments to Doreen, "This is going to be quite a journey for the organization. And, if I may say, for you. It's a bigger change than you can appreciate, at this point in the journey."

Doreen replies, "I expect that you're right. I'm glad that we have your experience to help us, but I know that we will have to find our own way." And in that moment, she realized that she needed to take notes along the way, both to organize her thoughts and to help her to look back on where the organization had been and how it changed over time.

Leaders are formed in crucibles of extreme change for which one is never fully prepared. There are no warm-up act, no safety net, and no second chances. There are also no experts to consult, no "best practices" to adopt. These crises are rough-and-tumble, hands-on, hold-on-to-your-hat rides that demand the best of people, and in return, help to develop people in ways that they could not have imagined.

Leaders are formed in crucibles of extreme change for which one is never fully prepared.

Leaders are essential catalysts who help their organizations adapt to changing conditions. Leading change, especially during existential crises, is their fundamental purpose; it is what separates leadership from management. Management deals with maintaining and improving an existing, working organization. Leadership, in contrast, deals with creating a new organization, and a new culture, sometimes from nothing, but often from the wreckage of an earlier organization that was no longer capable of meeting new challenges. Leadership is, fundamentally, about confronting the unknown and growing the organization's ability to deal with it.

Change can be intimidating, even paralyzing. Dealing with the unknown is never easy, but ignoring it never makes it go away. The only way to move ahead is to plunge right in, keep your eyes open, ask a lot of questions, and be prepared to try different approaches, examine the results, and adapt based on the new information. The case study explores how a large, traditional organization learns how to pivot by changing its culture and the company's explicit and implicit reward system to embrace empiricism and transparency.

REDUCING DEPENDENCIES MAKES CHANGE POSSIBLE

> Not long after the company call, Carl (the head of Reliable Energy's project management office [PMO]) reaches out to Doreen and Nagesh to discuss how the new business unit will be integrated into the other work being done in the organization. He asks Nagesh for his product roadmap, with milestones, saying that this will be essential to help coordinate the new initiative with other projects and programs under way.
>
> Nagesh pushes back, saying that's not how his organization and its members work. They don't have a product roadmap, but they have goals that he will share. He explains that they work with agile practices: make short releases toward those goals, measure the results, then adapt their strategies and goals as needed. They will be fully transparent about their goals and what they learn from releases, but they can't plan out their releases in detail because they learn important information from each release that would mean that any long-term product plans would be a waste of effort.
>
> Carl is somewhat amused by this and responds dismissively: "It might be fine for a small start-up to run itself that way, but Reliable Energy is a huge organization that spends hundreds of millions every year on projects, most of which interconnect and have impacts on each other. We simply can't run a 'grown-up' organization like a bunch of kids."
>
> Nagesh responds, "Actually, you can run a large organization that way. And many very successful large organizations do run this way today—at least in the parts of the organization that are developing new products and services. ..."

Doreen jumps in. "Carl, I understand your concerns, but we're not going to force Nagesh's team to work in the way we've always done and risk losing the unique value that they're creating. We bought their company to learn from them, and so we need to let them work in the way that makes the most sense for them."

Carl is unconvinced and shows annoyance. "How are we going to coordinate between different projects without coordinating project plans? We have enough trouble now with teams dropping features at the last minute, which creates a domino effect among all the projects that depend on them. Only with diligent oversight from my PMO are we able to make sure that everyone is on track."

Nagesh offers his solution. "Our team publishes interfaces to our product that we faithfully honor. If we put a feature in our published interface, that interface won't change; we guarantee that it will work in all subsequent releases. We run tests against every release to make sure of it. And when we add new features, we update our interfaces and honor them. By doing that, we're able to work with other companies without having to coordinate our schedules. You could do the same."

Dependencies are the enemies of change. Many organizations are so internally intertwined that they can't change even small things without breaking lots of other things. They try to manage complexity with more planning, which does expose the dependencies, but changing within the constraints imposed by these dependencies requires such execution finesse that the pace of change slows to a crawl.

Dependencies are the enemies of change.

The best way to manage dependencies is to eliminate them. One way to do so is to implement stable, defined interfaces between products or different parts of the organization. Doing so enables different parts of the organization to change the way they work without disrupting others. It also helps organizations create partner ecosystems by providing ways to build value-added products and services on top of existing products. As a result, interfaces have become an integral part of most new-product strategies. Coordinating activities and dependencies across products slow everyone down to the speed of the slowest team. Interfaces sever these dependencies and let different teams move at the pace that best matches their needs and abilities.

Organizations can reduce complexity in several ways. Using shared architectures or platforms, as the teams in the case study propose to do, is one way to achieve this. Another way is to simplify the products themselves. Most products are complex collections of features that serve many different groups of people. By using a shared product architecture and breaking complex products into simpler products that serve a smaller, more cohesive group of people, organizations can reduce the dependencies between products so that instead of depending on many other products, each product depends only on the shared product platform.[1]

NOT EVERYONE MAY NEED TO CHANGE, AT LEAST AT FIRST

> In the weeks after the acquisition announcement, Nagesh finds himself swamped with requests to talk to various managers and teams about what his organization is doing, to learn more about how they work. While he appreciates the good intentions behind these requests, they divert his attention from supporting and growing his team and their product.
>
> He talks to Doreen about this problem. She understands that these managers are afraid of missing out on something important, and while their eagerness to learn is a positive sign, there are better ways to satisfy their curiosity without interrupting Nagesh and his team. She contacts an agile coach with whom Nagesh has worked and asks the coach to run a series of workshops for managers to help them understand agility and empiricism, and to help them decide whether it would help them and whether they are ready for it.

While the entire organization needs to develop a new business model, it can't simply pivot to the new model immediately; it has existing customers and suppliers that depend on the old business model, at least at the present time.

---

1. For more about this approach, see www.pragmaticinstitute.com/resources/articles/product/untangling-products-focus-on-desired-outcomes-to-decrease-product-complexity/.

Forcing the entire organization to change and potentially damaging the existing model is as dangerous as failing to develop a new business model to replace the one that will inevitably fade. Being mindful of who needs to change, and why, is the starting point for the discussion on how to change, and when. People struggle to adapt when they aren't sure why they need to be agile.

Doreen joins the first of these workshops to share what she thinks the organization needs to do to become more responsive to changes in the market. "We need to improve our delivery speed, increase our productivity, better respond to changing priorities, and improve alignment across the organization. That's what agility and responsiveness mean to me."

Nagesh, who has also joined the workshop, says, "All those things were and are important to my organization, but we learned something as we delivered faster and measured the result: We were able to get closer to our customers by getting faster feedback. As a result, we were able to try new ideas faster, gather feedback, and in a lot of cases, to stop doing things that weren't important to customers. We also had to deal with a chronic 'knowledge shortage'—because we were constantly evolving what we were building and how we were building it, we never had enough 'experts' to answer all their questions. We had to learn how to learn together, and to be self-sufficient and self-managing, so as to survive and thrive."

Doreen has to think about this, but realizes that Nagesh is right. As an organization, Reliable Energy doesn't really know what its customers really need, but the only way it will learn is to deliver something to those customers and get feedback.

"Those are great observations, Nagesh. We've tried simply asking customers what they want in the past, and we often find that when we deliver to them what they want, what we delivered wasn't what they really needed. We had the opportunity to learn something, but because we had invested a lot of time and money in building something that didn't meet their needs, we usually had to move on to other things and so missed opportunities to learn. Ultimately, we need to get closer to our customers to learn from them much faster than we do today. Delivering faster is a part of that, but it's not really the goal."

Many organizations state that their reason for wanting to improve their agility and responsiveness is to "go faster" or "deliver faster," but this doesn't really tell the whole story. Those organizations that measure the value that they deliver to their customers by gathering feedback often find that they have a lot of misconceptions about what customers really need. Sometimes, they find that customers also don't understand what they need.

At first, these organizations may be shocked, because they thought that their stakeholders had a deep understanding of customers' needs. Once they overcome this shock, they can see that a lot of what they had planned to deliver isn't useful—and this knowledge frees them to pursue things from which customers will derive more benefit.

When dealing with a world that is changing rapidly, the only way to learn what is really needed is often to try things and see if they will work. The art of doing this is to experiment quickly, and with the smallest investment needed to learn. Traditional organizations make too many expensive assumptions and then take too long to test them. They think they have to have all the answers, and change everything at once.

In a complex world, organizations usually don't know what needs to change. Because they need to learn by taking many small, quick steps, not everyone needs to change all at once. But who does need to change? That answer is simple: the people who are going to run the controlled learning experiments.

As the organization learns, more and more teams will find over time that they need to more directly engage with customers to test assumptions and learn more about what customers need. But the learning will be slow at first, and will involve a small number of teams, because at first the organization won't even know which questions to ask or how to frame experiments. Each team needs time to form and to learn a new way of working. In short, they need to learn how to learn. Before teams can improve their time to deliver, they first have to focus on decreasing their time to learn.

NOT EVERYONE SEES COMPLEXITY THE SAME WAY

Carl approaches Doreen after one of these workshops. "Doreen, with all due respect, I don't find this 'experiential learning' stuff very compelling. We've known for years that our problems are mostly a matter of not executing our plans very well. At the start of every project and program we identify risks and assumptions, and we develop mitigation plans to deal with the challenges that come up. How is our current situation any different? In the past, we've fallen down when we didn't actually use those risk mitigation plans and people just started improvising. I feel that you are giving license to letting people just make up things on the fly. ..."

"Carl, I appreciate what you are saying, but that's simply not the case. Remember the smart grid pilot we ran 8 years ago? We made a lot of assumptions about the willingness of people to pay for the cost of upgrading their infrastructure, which turned out to be wrong. Ultimately, we had to kill the project, but we spent a lot of money before we learned that our assumptions were flawed.

"Our problem, as I see it, is not that we fail to plan, but that we plan too much based on assumptions or too little information. We need to get better at making small bets and getting better information, faster. That's what we're trying to do here."

Carl's experiences color his perceptions. He believes that with enough up-front information, plans for solving problems and delivering solutions can be developed and executed. His beliefs about the "right way to manage" shape his approach to planning: Problems are understood, an approach is defined, the right practices are selected, a plan is created, and then the organization's execution of that plan is monitored. Carl's approach assumes that the plan is right, and deviations from the plan are indications that corrective action is required.

Some people believe that many of the same benefits that agility promises—namely, delivering faster with less waste—can be achieved by better planning, and that plans are essential to coordinating the activity of large numbers of people. And when requirements and assumptions are correct and stable, Carl's approach is perfectly reasonable. But when everything is in flux, the plan-centric approach falls apart. Many of the most challenging problems that organizations face today are novel and complex, and this novelty defies attempts to use our experiences of cause and effect to create plans that lead to effective solutions.[2]

When everything is in flux, the plan-centric approach falls apart.

Changing someone's view of the world is difficult, if not impossible, at least from the outside. People must experience the world in a different way to change the way they look at it. They have formed their belief system based on their experience, and it takes a lot of countervailing evidence to change it. Arguing with them that their approach isn't working usually causes them to dig in and double-down on their position.

ORGANIZATIONAL CHANGE REQUIRES PROTECTIVE, PROGRESSIVE DICTATORSHIP

> Doreen continues, "Carl, I appreciate your concerns, but in this case I feel that we need to learn a new way to learn. We don't know enough about the challenges ahead to make effective plans, so, at least for our work on developing a new business model, we are going to let Nagesh's organization work in a different way. We will take what they learn and apply it where it makes sense in the rest of the organization. I don't see any other way to move ahead."

The irony of agile organizational transformation is that while eventually the people in the organization will need to learn to become more self-managing and collaborative when they make decisions, the early stages of the change require the agile leader to be somewhat dictatorial. That person needs to create a space in which people can experiment and learn, even while some other parts of the organization are trying to shut down the change.

---

2. Inspired by Dave Snowden, "The Cynefin framework": www.cognitive-edge.com/the-cynefin-framework/.

Different terms have been used to describe the "protected environments" in which new approaches can be tried without interference from the rest of the organization: skunk works, innovation labs, incubators, and the like.[3] The key enabler of these environments is a progressive, politically powerful executive who charters the organization to achieve a mission, provides the organization with the resources that it needs to survive, and, most importantly, protects the group from outside tampering.

The "incubator" or "innovation center" metaphor that is usually applied to these groups is actually misguided when trying to use them as mechanisms to change the organization. On the one hand, incubators usually produce a prototype, which then needs to be transitioned into some steady-state existing organization. Calling this group an incubator suggests that what it's doing is not really "ready for the real world"—and that's not the case with agile change.

On the other hand, while promoting innovation is a good thing, the term "innovation center" can result in a belief that innovation has to happen in some special group to be legitimate. In reality, opportunities for innovation arise everywhere in most organizations.

In the case of agile transformation, what really should happen is that the so-called innovation center is actually exploring and refining a new way of working that will eventually need to be replicated in other areas of the organization. For this reason, the term "agile cell" best describes how these early agile teams should be regarded—as cells that ultimately need to reproduce and spread through the organization. But more about this later.

---

3. For an example, see this description of the Scrum Studio: www.scrum.org/resources/scrum-studio-model-innovation.

TWO PATHS, ONE GOAL

> Doreen reflects on her discussions with Carl. She recognizes that not everyone in the organization wants to change, or needs to. Carl's concerns are probably shared by many other members of the organization, and at least Carl is being open about them. Keeping the existing organization focused on delivering value to existing customers while exploring new alternatives really does require two very different organizations with very different operating models; running one organization with one operating model is tough enough. Yet she remains convinced that letting Nagesh and other teams work on rapidly learning and adapting is the right way to start to change the organization. Carl and the "traditional" organization need to stay focused on the work that is familiar and stable, and also important to the success of the organization, but even they will need to learn how to learn faster over time.
>
> As a compromise, Doreen decides that the agile teams will provide transparency into what they are doing. Doreen and other stakeholders will participate in their reviews, but they will not be subject to the governance model imposed by the traditional organization. Carl's PMO will continue to oversee the work done by the rest of the organization.
>
> Doreen brings Carl and Nagesh together to communicate her decision. Carl objects because he feels his authority is being undermined. Doreen privately wonders whether his real concern is with his status in the organization, but he ultimately accepts that it is her decision to make and agrees. Doreen realizes that Carl is going to be a challenge to manage, but for now his agreement is all she needs.

Existing organizations face a challenge that start-ups don't: They need to support the current business, even if they realize that their current business may be going away and they need to develop a new business model.[4] In response, creating dual, parallel organizations is one way that they try to do both.

The key challenge for the agile leader is to make it permissible to work in different ways so long as everyone is working toward the same goal. Minimizing dependencies, as noted earlier in this chapter, is one way to minimize the

---

4. Inspired by John Kotter's discussion of how traditional organizational hierarchies evolve: www.kotterinc.com/book/accelerate/.

conflicts and complexities of coordinating work being done by teams working in different ways (see Figure 1.1).

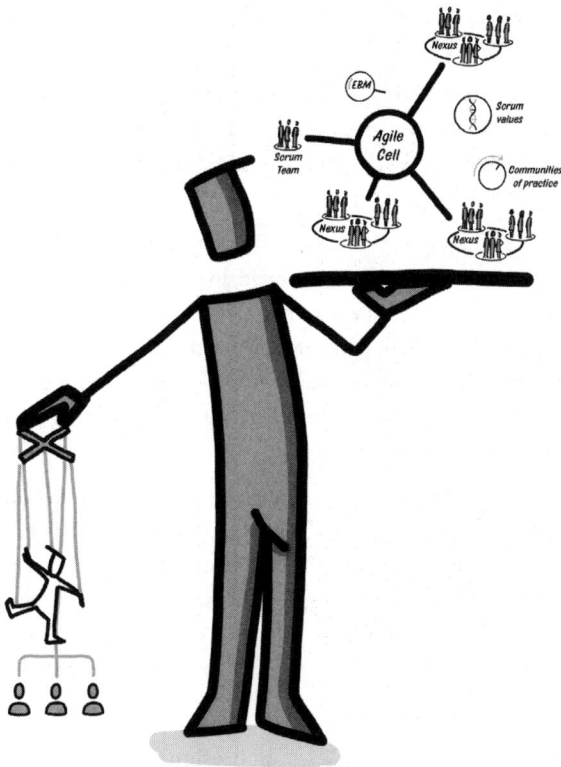

Figure 1.1 Supporting two different operating models helps organizations to balance agile and traditional approaches.

Later, in a discussion with Doreen about having two "operating models" for the organization, Nagesh observes an important difference between the two operating models:

- The traditional model is largely built upon individual performance and rewards.

- The empirical model can only thrive when the organization values and rewards teamwork and collaboration.

"This has a big impact on how performance is rewarded and how people view their careers. We don't have to deal with the problem at the moment, but we will before we can scale this effort much beyond a few teams. We were starting to deal with this issue at Energy Bridge, but since all employees had stock options they were willing to suspend their concerns. Now we are starting to get questions from people about 'Where is all this leading, for me?'"

Doreen nods. "I think for now we have to focus on figuring out how these teams are going to work, and protect and support this new way of working. But, yes, we will need to work out how this impacts the employees' perceptions of their career opportunities."

Nagesh agrees, "For now, we should be aware that people in these two different kinds of organizations view their world in very different terms. We see this in Carl's response to complexity: His response to the unknown is to plan and monitor more rigorously. This belief is deeply held and widely shared. But people experienced with empiricism know that the only way to reduce complexity is to learn more and faster. This requires framing hypotheses, running experiments, gathering data, and learning from the results."

Doreen adds, "Yes, but we can't change everyone at once, and some people will never change. For now, we need to literally keep the lights on while we work out new ways of working in your agile cell. You and I, and others in agile leadership roles, have to bridge the gap between these two ways of working while we help the organization to grow and adapt."

Every existing organization faces a challenge when evolving a radically new way of working: keeping the existing organization focused on serving its existing customers and sustaining the revenues on which it depends. People in the old/traditional part of the organization need to focus on keeping the train running while the organization experiments with new approaches in new areas, or in old areas that have already been disrupted.

The challenge for leaders is that the very act of trying new approaches, even in isolated parts of the organization, is threatening to people in the old organization when it creates fear in them of losing their jobs, their influence, or their status in the long term. Even when they recognize that the organization needs to change, they may resist that change on a personal level because it might cause them to lose something important to them.

The challenge for agile leaders is to understand and respect the perceived threats to the traditional parts of their organizations while creating space in which new approaches can be tried out and refined based on experience. Balancing these two competing forces, and actually aligning them so that both work toward the same goal, is an art that takes practice to master. Exploring approaches that help agile leaders to develop these skills is a major focus of subsequent chapters.

REFLECTIONS ON THE JOURNEY

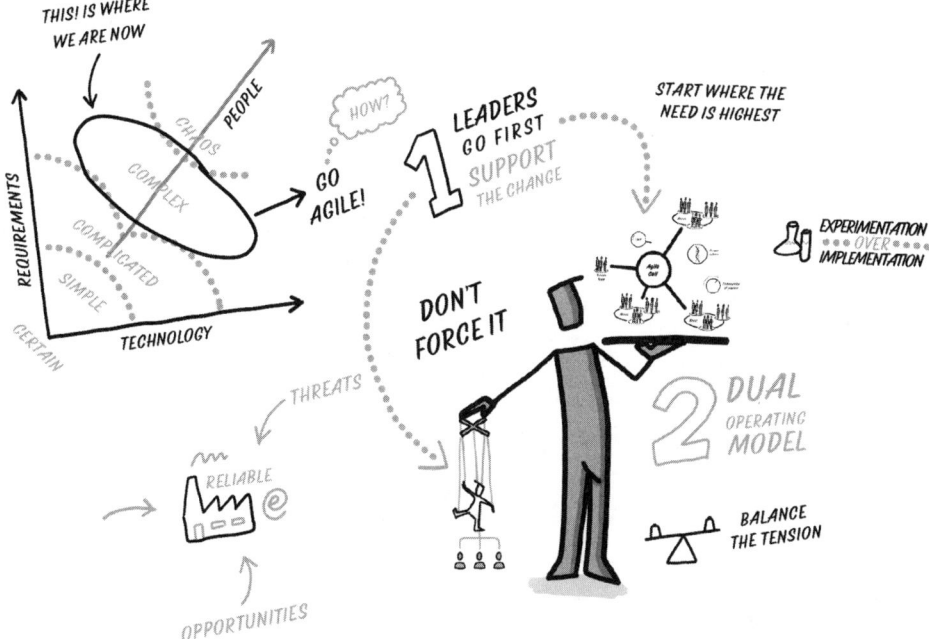

Organizations seek agility as a way to overcome the challenges they face. When dealing with complex problems, where there are no sure answers and the proven methods of the past are failing, the only successful approach is to take small steps toward goals, measure the results, and then adapt based on what the organization learns.

This doesn't mean trying to change the whole organization at once. Instead, the organization can choose the area in which it faces the greatest challenge and start there, learning as it goes. This requires a subtle balancing act—keeping the existing organization moving forward while actively trying new approaches that are deliberately trying to find new ways of working. Ultimately, the organization will have to choose which way it goes, but at the start it simply needs to create an environment in which it can try new things and learn.

FORMING TEAMS AND DISCOVERING PURPOSE

Empowered cross-functional teams are the agile organization's engines for creating customer value. Agile leaders play a critical role in creating the right conditions for these teams to take ownership. By enabling teams to form themselves, leaders set the tone and expectations for teams' self-management and accountability.

Unfortunately, many traditional leaders send the wrong message from the start. They determine what the organization is going to deliver (their product or service), then decide the process by which the organization is going to deliver the product, and finally form teams to follow the predefined process to deliver the predefined product. The result is disengaged teams who passively follow a process to deliver products and services that don't meet customer needs. Sound familiar?

As they help teams to form, agile leaders also help those teams discover their purpose, thereby enabling them to focus on the customers and their desired outcomes. Rather than dictating solutions to teams, agile leaders give the teams permission to better understand their customers and devise innovative solutions that meet their needs, and then refine these solutions using delivery-feedback loops.

CHANGING THE ORGANIZATION, ONE TEAM AT A TIME

A few days after the announcement of the acquisition of Energy Bridge, Doreen and Nagesh are discussing their next steps. Doreen wants to start building on what Energy Bridge has started and thinks their next step should be to have Nagesh run a series of educational workshops, first with company executives, and then expanding to all the teams within Reliable Energy, to help them understand what agility can bring to them.

"Our people are really excited to learn more about what these changes could mean for them and their teams. We need to capture that excitement, and channel it, while we have the chance. I'm also starting to hear murmurings about people fearing what this might mean for their jobs. We have to get out in front of that before rumors start."

"I appreciate your excitement and concerns about sharing information with people, and we do need to respond to their desire to know more about working in an agile way," Nagesh begins, "but we have to carefully manage their expectations about change. A little knowledge can be dangerous, and too much information, before they are ready to apply it, will only confuse them.

"Let me share an experience I had at another company some years ago. We did exactly what you describe, a series of internal sessions to educate people about agility and agile ways of working. Some people said, 'Oh, that's what agile is; we've been doing that for years,' even though they really hadn't. They were simply projecting their own misconceptions onto what they heard.

"Other people got very excited to work in a new way. They felt stifled and constrained in their current work, and they were eager to be part of what they considered 'the future of the company.' But the organization was not ready for them to work in a different way; they needed them to keep working on their existing projects until they had delivered. The disappointment of having their hopes raised and then dashed was very demoralizing.

"Other teams decided to 'try some agile techniques,' but because they were not consistent about their work and lacked guidance from experienced people, they struggled to achieve anything valuable. They gradually abandoned their efforts, saying that 'they had tried agile but it didn't work for them.'

"Finally, some managers began to realize that their authority would be undermined by this new way of working, and they began to quietly but deliberately resist the change.

The result of all this was that after about a year and a half, everyone was so frustrated with the lack of progress that the entire effort collapsed."

Doreen nodded in gradual understanding. "Yes, I can see how all those things could happen here. In fact, some of those things are already happening here, as team members go to conferences or read articles and try to bring new ideas to their teams. But we have to move forward—what should we do?"

"When we started Energy Bridge, we determined that we were going to do things differently. Because we were a start-up, we didn't have an existing organization to dismantle and rebuild, but the way we started new teams can work for us here.

"When we wanted to expand into a new market, we formed a new team from a combination of new hires and existing employees who volunteered because they wanted to try something different. The existing employees provided the 'seed' of the culture we wanted to establish, and they then ran the hiring process to recruit new team members. Every new team member had to have the unanimous support of all existing team members."

"That must have taken a lot of time."

"It can, but it actually took less time than if I'd been doing the hiring. Since we had several people looking at candidates, interviews could take place in parallel. The advantage is that the interviewing process reinforced team-building and built commitment to support new hires once they joined the team."

"I'll have to see how that works, but it sounds intriguing. Where do you think we can use that approach?"

"We've talked about our need to do something in the area of grid-scale energy storage. That's probably batteries, in our case, but some utilities are doing it by pumping water to higher reservoirs to store energy. We don't have expertise in that area, and the industry as a whole is still finding its way. Since there are no 'experts' to hire, I suggest we form a team around that need.

"By helping the team form in the right way, and then supporting them as they learn how to work together, we will set a powerful example of how agility will work in the broader organization. By being transparent about what they are learning, we will help others in the organization learn how agility will work here. As the organization discovers new areas where it needs agility, we can repeat this pattern."

"I like it. And we do need to solve the grid-scale energy storage problem... ."

"Getting the right people and the right chemistry is more important than getting the right idea."

—Ed Catmull[1]

While organizations are often tempted to aim for broad adoption of agile techniques, they are rarely rewarded with success. What begins with well-intentioned sharing tends to end in unfocused, watered-down superficial agility that does not build a foundation for success. The fundamental building block of an agile organization is the strong, empowered, self-managing team. Building such teams takes time and conscious investment, protection from hostile forces, and support and nurturing for a new way of working. Forming new teams around new initiatives, staffed by people who actually crave a new approach to their work and their teammates, is the best way to start fresh, unburdened by existing team member dynamics, roles, and processes.

The worst approach is to try to change an existing team or department, which already has solidified working relationships and behavior patterns. Changing the way of working inevitably changes team dynamics and threatens status relationships. While breaking up existing teams may seem costly and unproductive, trying to change the way an existing team works is nearly impossible; there are simply too many entrenched behavior patterns standing in the way.

The second worst approach is to assign people to new teams,[2] some of whom will see no reason to change. Forcing people to change is always a bad idea; a better approach is to find people who want to change, invite them to form new teams, and then help them, rather than trying to convince people who are resistant to change to work in a different way. Some organizations try to facilitate change by hiring external coaches to catalyze the change, but having

---

1. Ed Catmull and Amy Wallace, *Creativity, Inc.: Overcoming the Unseen Forces That Stand in the Way of True Inspiration* (Random House, 2014).

2. Even with their consent. The mere act of asking someone to do something can be coercive. People naturally want to please others, especially those in positions of authority, and the act of asking someone usually comes with a tacit expression that the person asking thinks it is a good idea. Employees may not feel they can say "no" without suffering negative consequences.

to work with people who don't want to change in the first place already puts them at a disadvantage.

Using external coaches is not necessarily a bad idea (each of the authors has played this role from time to time), but external coaches are expensive and good ones are hard to find. There is also a limit to what someone from outside the team can do to help a team change and grow. They can help a team to learn new approaches quickly, but they can also become a crutch that prevents the team from becoming accountable for their own growth. When you do need to use coaches, do so with the intention of making them superfluous as soon as possible. When they do, move them on to help another team, and so on.

This approach is much more effective than what many organizations do: hire lots of external coaches and spread them thin across too many teams. When the organization takes this path, the teams get frustrated because they aren't progressing, the coaches get frustrated because they are achieving little impact for the efforts, and executives in the organization are frustrated because they see little return on the money they are spending. Such an approach damages trust and often leaves members of the organization demoralized and believing that the organization is incapable of change. It may indeed be incapable of change, but it's not the fault of the coaches; it's the overall approach. You can't outsource change.

> *"People don't resist change. They resist being changed."*
>
> —Peter Senge

Shortcutting Team Formation Won't Produce Faster Results

Impatient executives often complain that changing an organization incrementally, on a team-by-team basis, is too slow. They want fast results and want to believe that their chosen "transformation" approach will bring more rapid changes and improvements in results. That would certainly be nice, but the reality is that no approach works faster than building strong, high-performing teams. Believing that such an approach exists is actually a dangerous fantasy, one that prevents leaders from getting started on the admittedly hard work of building high-performing teams.

Unfortunately, the term "agile transformation" also encourages magical thinking: It suggests that outside consultants can bring some set of training classes, workshops, and facilitated sessions to an organization that will change that organization overnight. While training classes, workshops, and the like are most assuredly important tools in transferring knowledge, they can't change deeply ingrained behavior patterns that people have developed over the course of years. People are very adaptable to change, but they have to change themselves, with the right environment and leadership; no one can do it for them.

FINDING THE RIGHT PEOPLE

Based on Nagesh's experiences, Doreen and Nagesh put out a call to employees to volunteer to join the new Grid-Scale Storage (GSS) team in the agile cell. Nagesh has explained to Doreen that it's much easier to get people to work in a new way when they are the ones who make the choice to change, and that forcing people to change almost never works.

There is a lot of interest in joining the team. Some volunteers are simply interested in doing something new, and others in better understanding what it means to be "agile." But some people also have a passion for the problems the team will need to solve: A few people have electric vehicles (EVs), a few have solar panels on their own homes, and one person even used to work for a wind turbine manufacturer.

A couple of Energy Bridge team members also volunteer to work on the new team. They feel the best way to make sure that the culture they value continues to thrive and grow is to help this new team form and work in a new way.

To help the team come together, Doreen and Nagesh make some initial decisions about team membership based on the interviews, which are led mostly by Nagesh. In those interviews, he explores the views of the potential team members about dealing with uncertainty and working as team members; their attitudes toward trust and transparency; and their experiences working as a member of a team. This excludes a few people who seem to be motivated simply by a desire for novelty and a few others who seem to be simply trying to build their resume. This leaves Doreen and Nagesh with just short of 20 potential candidates.

The Ideal Team Player

In his book *The Ideal Team Player*, Patrick Lencioni observes that people who thrive on teams and contribute most to the team's success have three qualities (see Figure 2.1).

Building upon Lencioni's *The Ideal Team Player*:

Humility

No excessive ego or concerns about status

Points out others' contributions and avoids seeking own attention

Emphasizes team over individual success

Hunger

Always looking for more to do, more to learn, and more responsibility

Self-motivated

Sustainable commitment and going beyond when required

Smart (Emotional Intelligence)

Aware of group dynamics

Asks good questions

Empathic listener

Engages in conversations

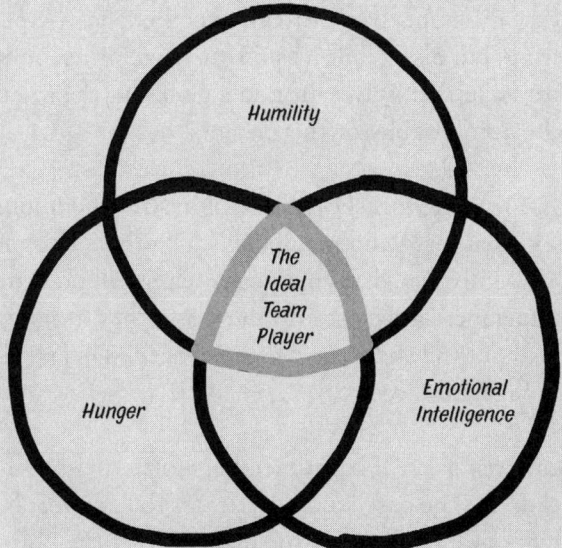

Figure 2.1 The ideal team player displays a combination of humility, hunger, and emotional intelligence.

These qualities select for people who are flexible and have demonstrated both the desire and the ability to work with others to solve problems. Using these criteria may exclude some otherwise high-performing individuals who are skilled but less willing or able to work as team members. The ideal team consists not of individual high performers, as some traditional managers might believe, but rather good, solid performers who know how to channel their energies into helping the entire team perform better.

> Nagesh looks over the list of candidate team members and says, "This is a great starting point. We can get a couple of people from Energy Bridge to act as facilitators and run a workshop to let team members choose the team they want to work on. We'll start by having the group identify the kinds of skills that they think each team will need, and then have candidates volunteer themselves to work on one team or the other, based on their skills, the kind of things they want to work on, and the people they want to work with. It takes some give-and-take, but it's a great way to start engaging the team by empowering them to choose their own teammates."

Team self-selection can unleash the passion and intrinsic motivation of the team members, and it sends a clear message that working on the new team will be very different than the team members have experienced before. It is empowering, but also reinforces the message of accountability: Teams are allowed to form themselves around a goal, but the organization expects that team to be accountable for their results.

The team-forming workshop also emphasizes the importance of having a balance of skills across team members, which the team members achieve by discussing the skills that they think each team will need to be successful. Since the team members are closest to the work, they are the best people to make decisions about the skills the team will need. This is a big change for traditional managers to accept.

You might even ask, "If team members form their own teams, what is the role of the leader?" The case study illustrates the answer: Nagesh and Doreen establish the overall goals for the team and set the boundary conditions for how team formation will work. In addition to solving certain customer-related problems (e.g., energy generation and storage), they indicate that they want the teams to form so that the skills of each team are broad and deep enough to achieve the team's goals.

The skills needed may vary from team to team, and establishing the connection between skills and goal achievement helps to counter the tendency for teams to become homogeneous with respect to their skill and personality composition. Team members need diversity in both aspects to be creative and continuously challenge each other. For example, without a nudge from the leaders, extraverted team members may choose people like themselves and miss out on having more diverse viewpoints from members who are more introverted but think deeply about a problem and possible solutions.

Empowering Diversity, Equality, and Inclusion

Diverse teams tend to perform better than homogeneous teams.[3] As part of helping agile teams to self-organize, agile leaders have both the opportunity and the responsibility to help them embrace diversity, equality, and inclusion. The challenge for agile leaders is to do this without harming the team's ability to self-organize and self-manage.

Leaders in traditional organizations tend to make team membership decisions, so it is easier for them to simply select people for membership on a team in ways that help to improve—at least in theory—the diversity of the team. But deciding team membership is one of the ways that teams start to learn to self-manage. Telling the team who will be on the team, no matter how well-intentioned a gesture, undercuts the team's ability to self-manage.

Instead of making inclusion decisions for the team, agile leaders need to coach potential team members on the value and importance of diverse teams that promote equality between team members, and that strive to be inclusive of different backgrounds and perspectives. Leaders can do so by asking powerful questions of the team as it is forming that help the team self-assess their own team composition by making potential diversity concerns transparent, and then deciding as a team how to resolve concerns.

Teams who are new to self-managing need more help from agile leaders to strike the right balance. Agile leaders, in turn, need to hone their coaching and indirect influencing skills to help teams learn and grow in their ability to form diverse teams.

3. For more on this topic, see www.psychologytoday.com/us/blog/your-brain-work/202106/why-diverse-teams-outperform-homogeneous-teams.

EMPOWERING TEAMS

During the interviews, Nagesh heard a few of the Reliable Energy volunteers express that they feel the company has a culture that is toxic to change. They want to work in a more creative way, and they don't see how that can happen in a culture that punishes "failure." Carl is not mentioned by name, but one of his catchphrases, "one throat to choke," is cited as evidence of a culture that punishes unexpected results. They want assurances that the new team will work differently.

Nagesh brings up this point to Doreen afterward, but without mentioning Carl by name: "If we have done a good job empowering the teams, they will hold themselves accountable for the *outcomes* they deliver, but we understand that the path to these outcomes is uncertain. We don't want to punish teams for encountering the unexpected; we want them to learn from the new information and adapt as they seek toward their goal."

Nagesh continues: "Giving them the freedom to try new things and to learn is an important part of empowerment. We are telling them we trust them to do what they need to do to deliver the results we would like to achieve. If we want them to hold themselves accountable, we have to give them the freedom to find their own way."

Doreen reflects on what the employees and Nagesh have shared. "I hadn't really thought about it in that way before, and how our traditional way of holding people accountable is based on activities and outputs, not outcomes. By switching to outcomes, we can hold the teams accountable for real results, not arbitrary items on a plan."

Traditional organizations manage people to a plan; deviations from the plan indicate that something has gone "off track." The problem with this approach in a complex world is that it might be the plan that is wrong and the team that is doing the right thing. In fact, most plans are based on scant information and are prepared by people who, although they are doing their best, are just guessing about the right thing to do.

Managing to a plan feels comfortable because it allows an organization to measure activities and outputs, but leads to a false sense of security that it's doing the right thing. The problem is that those activities and outputs often have nothing to do with actually achieving the results the organization wants. So what's the alternative? Measure outcomes delivered directly, but do it frequently, and inspect and adapt based on the new information obtained.

Empowering a team to make its own decisions about how to reach a goal is really the foundation of empowerment. And since the team members are closest to the work itself, they are usually in the best position to make decisions about what work they should do and how to do it. But with this decision-making freedom comes accountability for delivering the customer outcomes that form the basis for the team's goals.[4]

With decision-making freedom comes accountability for delivering customer outcomes.

The Role of Intrinsic Motivation in Team Performance

In his book *Drive: The Surprising Truth About What Motivates Us*, Dank Pink cites three elements of motivation: autonomy, mastery, and purpose.[5] Pink's thesis, in brief, is that for anything but simple, mechanical tasks, providing people with the autonomy to manage their own work, rewarding them for achieving mastery, and motivating them with compelling goals achieves far greater results than traditional management approaches.

---

4. We cover empowerment and delegation strategies and techniques in greater depth in Chapter 4. The purpose of the techniques discussed there is to establish clear boundaries for a team, arrived at through mutual agreement between leaders and agile teams. These "guardrails" help the team to grow their self-management while respecting that they are usually still learning how to effectively self-manage.

5. See www.danpink.com/books/drive/ and www.youtube.com/watch?v=y1SDV8nxypE for more information about Dan Pink's insights into motivation.

Based on research on its teams, Google found the following factors most contributed to team effectiveness:[6]

Psychological safety. Psychological safety refers to an individual's perception of the consequences of taking an interpersonal risk or a belief that a team is safe for risk taking in the face of being seen as ignorant, incompetent, negative, or disruptive. In a team with high psychological safety, teammates feel safe to take risks around their team members. They feel confident that no one on the team will embarrass or punish anyone else for admitting a mistake, asking a question, or offering a new idea.

Dependability. On dependable teams, members reliably complete quality work on time (versus the opposite—shirking responsibilities).

Structure and clarity. An individual's understanding of job expectations, the process for fulfilling these expectations, and the consequences of one's performance are important for team effectiveness. Goals can be set at the individual or group level and must be specific, challenging, and attainable. Google often uses Objectives and Key Results (OKRs) to help set and communicate short- and long-term goals.

Meaning. Finding a sense of purpose in either the work itself or the output is important for team effectiveness. The meaning of work is personal and can vary. It might be financial security, supporting one's family, helping the team succeed, or self-expression for each individual, for example.

Impact. The results of their work, the subjective judgment that their work is making a difference, is important for teams. Seeing that their work is contributing to the organization's goals can help reveal impact.

Traditional management has a self-fulfilling flaw: By assuming that people are not intrinsically motivated to do their best, and by micromanaging them using guess-work-based plans of activities and outputs, they guarantee that people will be unmotivated. At the same time, providing too much freedom without setting clear, outcome-based goals creates chaos and eventually leads to demotivation. Conversely, setting clear, ambitious outcome-based goals that capture people's imaginations provides people with purpose. By rewarding people for achieving those goals, and for the mastery and skill development that they must evolve to reach those goals, leaders motivate teams to achieve better results. And by demonstrating trust, these same leaders provide people with a sense of pride that amplifies their motivation.

---

6. https://rework.withgoogle.com/print/guides/5721312655835136/

PLACING THE CUSTOMER AT THE CENTER OF THE CHANGE

To kick things off and to help them start learning how to work as a team, Nagesh leads the new team members in a workshop to develop their mission. This task turns out to be more difficult than they expected, as the team members discover that they really don't understand "the customer" very well. In fact, there is not a single "customer," but rather many different customers with very different needs and experiences.

Nagesh introduces a technique for identifying different groups of customers to make it easier to see what each group wants from the solution. Through the course of their lively discussions, the team comes to understand that they actually have four different types of customers, with very different desired outcomes (see Figure 2.2).

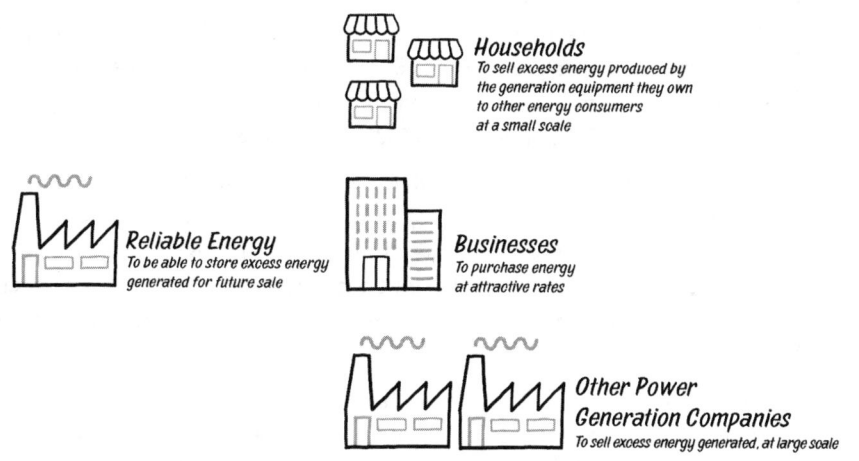

Households
To sell excess energy produced by the generation equipment they own to other energy consumers at a small scale

Reliable Energy
To be able to store excess energy generated for future sale

Businesses
To purchase energy at attractive rates

Other Power Generation Companies
To sell excess energy generated, at large scale

Figure 2.2 Customer groups and their desired outcomes, as identified by the Grid-Scale Storage (GSS) team.

Nagesh then asks a deeper question: "Where do you think each kind of customer is today, relative to where they would like to be? We can think of the difference between where they are today and where they would like to be as a satisfaction gap." (See Figure 2.3.)

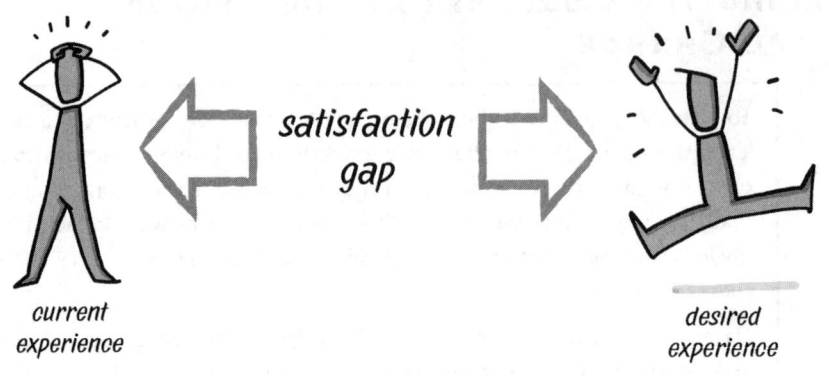

current
experience

satisfaction
gap

desired
experience

Figure 2.3 Targeting the gap between the current and desired experiences of different groups of customers helps teams to refine their goals.[7]

One of the team members chimes in: "Well, we don't measure those things today, but I think the gap is pretty large. But understanding customer needs in this way is interesting; it gives me a different way to think about what things we need to deliver to each of those different kinds of customers."

Nagesh has been listening for a while, and he chooses this moment to summarize something that the team has been gradually coming to understand: "Exactly. At Energy Bridge, we used these different satisfaction gaps to help us form our product goals, and to even give us ideas about what kinds of products and services we might need to deliver to help these different customers experience their desired outcomes."

Another team member reflects on this: "I have to say that, coming into this, I wondered whether this would be a good use of our time. I mean, we always talk about how we are a customer-focused company, and I thought we already understood our customers. But I am gradually seeing that our understanding was superficial. I think that looking at these satisfaction gaps gives us a better way to understand what we need to do and where we need to focus."

---

7. For more information about satisfaction gaps, see www.scrum.org/resources/blog/measure-business-opportunities-unrealized-value.

Another follows on: "Yes. I realize now that there is not one customer, but many different kinds of customers. The four we have identified here may not be the only ones we find, and we can add to this list over time. But being more attuned to each different group's satisfaction gaps gives us ways to talk about, and measure, needs that we didn't have before."

Teams need a powerful purpose to really come together; they need a mission that motivates them to make shared commitments to the organization and to each other to achieve that mission. They need to understand *why* they exist as a team. Expressing that *why* in terms of helping customers to achieve particular desired outcomes is the best way to really motivate team members.

Many teams think of their customers in terms of personas.[8] Some teams with which the authors have worked have even gone so far as to create posters of the customer personas and hang them on their team room walls to remind themselves of who they are really working for. This technique turns abstract discussions of customers into very focused discussions about what real customers really need.

It's easy to think of team formation as a two-step process: first form a great team (the *who*), and then point them toward an interesting problem to solve (the *why*). In reality, it's not so straightforward. The *why* influences the *who*, and vice versa. In the case study, many of the people who volunteered for the team had a deep personal interest in the problem that they presumed the team was going to solve. In turn, those people brought their insights into the discussion of who the customers are and what they want to achieve, which influenced the team mission.

Sometimes it takes a while to get this right. You start off thinking that the problem is one thing, but as the team delves deeper into the customers and their needs, you discover a different problem that changes who needs to be on the team. In addition, sometimes team members might think they want to

---

8. For more on how personas and outcomes can be used to simplify product definitions, see www.pragmaticinstitute.com/resources/articles/product/untangling-products-focus-on-desired-outcomes-to-decrease-product-complexity/.

work on a problem, but as their understanding of the problem grows, they may realize that they aren't as interested as they thought they were.

There is also another dynamic at work during this formative stage: The people on the team have to be able to work together. That doesn't mean that they all have to be great buddies, and they may not always agree; in fact, creative differences can power amazing team results. But they have to respect one another enough to be able to work through those differences, and some combinations of potential team members are just never going to work.

Leaders provide critical space and structure for the team to work through these dynamics. They nudge a little when necessary, but they don't dictate the final decisions. It's a challenging situation to "manage," because they want to grow the team's confidence in their own abilities by empowering them, but they also need to keep an eye on how the team dynamics are evolving. Do team members seem to be able to work together? Are they developing shared commitment around their team goals? Will achievement of those team goals contribute to their organization's ability to achieve its strategic goals?

There is a lot of uncertainty at first, and it's the leader's job to help the team to overcome those uncertainties, at least enough to start taking their first steps toward their goals (see Figure 2.4).

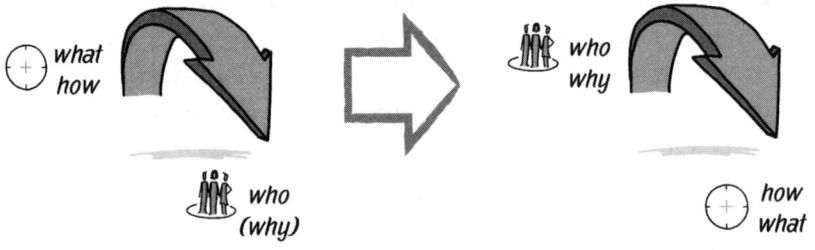

Figure 2.4 Helping teams to form starts with focusing on team membership (who) and team goals (why).

Figure 2.4 reveals a pattern that is often the key to a successful agile transformation: Start with the WHO (the right people with the right leadership skills) and combine that with the WHY (understanding your customers and turning that into a mission that everyone understands). Once the WHY and the WHO are filled in, it becomes much easier to make choices about HOW to create value and WHAT to do (and even more important, what *not* to do).

Many organizations approach agile change the other way around: They start with a portfolio, product backlogs, and agile processes; then they create an implementation strategy; and as a last step, they try to motivate everyone to take part in the change. No wonder, then, that people so often are not fully engaged in the change.

Chapter 3 explores how leaders help teams to discover *how* they are going to work and, in turn, *what* they are going to deliver to their customers.

TURNING CUSTOMER NEEDS INTO TEAM PURPOSE

> Reflecting on the customer outcomes workshop, Doreen gradually comes to a realization that she shares with Nagesh: "Watching how this team is coming together, I am beginning to realize how different this is from how we work today. In the rest of the organization, we tell people what they are going to work on, and what they are going to deliver, but we spend very little time talking about who we are really working for and what those customers need. I am beginning to realize we have it all backward. ... And we wonder why we have never seemed to achieve the results we thought we wanted!"
>
> Nagesh nods in agreement: "What I found in my prior companies was that it was very hard to change those ingrained patterns. I am glad you are open to trying a different way."

Doreen is quiet for a moment, and then observes: "What I really like about this approach is that it helps us to ground ourselves in customer needs. We make too many assumptions about what customers need, that turn out to be wrong. I also like that we are drawing people to the teams who are energized to work on customer problems. But ..."

Nagesh smiles. "I thought there was a 'but' coming."

Doreen smiles as well. "Not everything we work on is going to be so inspiring. We have a lot of things that need to get done that are a lot more mundane than developing a new product offering. How is it going to work then?"

"Let's come back to that question later. For now, we have a team that is making some excellent first steps, and we need to focus on helping them to be successful. And ... ," Nagesh pauses for effect, "let me just share that we are all social beings. We evolved to enjoy working together, if we create the right environment. My experience is that just the joy of working together toward a shared goal is enough, even if that goal is relatively mundane. Let's come back to that when we've had some more experiences with helping teams come together."

"Fair enough. But there is another thing that is bothering me. We don't have to solve this now, but I am beginning to understand that, as hard as it is, helping teams to form around a customer-focused mission is not our biggest problem. Our biggest problem is that you and I can only do so much. We are creating the space for this team to work in a new way, but we have a lot of old-school managers who are used to making decisions about who will work on a team and what that team will deliver. I now see that as wrong, but I don't know how to change those people. Yet."

"For now, for a while, you and I can create the space these new teams need. Over time, we will find other managers who want to grow in this new way and we can help them learn. But before we are done, we are going to find people who won't believe that this new way will work. If they won't change, we will need to help them find places inside or outside the organization where they can work in the way they think is best. The best thing we can do right now, however, is to show that this new way of doing things delivers better results—happier teams and happier customers."

REFLECTIONS ON THE JOURNEY

When leaders seek to make their organizations more agile, they often seek some sort of "shortcut" that can help the organization quickly change. In doing so, they fail to understand how embedded the existing way of doing things is in their organization. The only practical way for organizations to change is team-by-team. More than one team can be learning and changing at a time, if the leaders and the teams have enough bandwidth, so long as leaders help the teams to form and learn.

The starting point is to help teams to form from volunteers—that is, letting people choose who they work with and what they work on. Assigning people to teams and telling them what they are going to work on is the first false step many leaders make. The engine of agility is the self-managing team, and if the team members cannot be trusted to form their own teams, they will never be able to make the kind of complex decisions that they will need to make.

As these teams form, their values need to be focused on meeting unmet customer needs, expressed in terms of gaps between the customer's current experience and their desired experiences. Closing these satisfaction gaps will become the focus that gives the team purpose and provides them with the motivation they need to achieve great things.

SHIFTING FROM
OUTPUT TO IMPACT

At many organizations, members are accustomed to thinking about their organization's mission in manufacturing terms: They produce outputs that customers consume. Output-oriented organizations (whether those outputs are products or services) concern themselves with producing things quickly and efficiently, and as long as people buy those things they are happy.

The problem with this output-centric view is that people don't buy things for the sake of buying them (compulsive shoppers aside); they purchase goods and services because they believe that those items will help them achieve some particular outcome, such as solving a problem that they experience, alleviating a pain that they feel, or creating some sort of benefit that they realize. Considering what these customers are actually trying to achieve gives organizations insights into ways that they might be able to better serve customers. These insights may help the organization produce better products or services, or create wholly new products or services that may attract more customers.

Agile leaders help their organizations shift from focusing on outputs to focusing on impacts by framing goals in terms of customer outcomes instead of things that are produced (or worse, things that employees do). While this shift seems subtle, the results it produces are profound.

"WHAT GETS MEASURED GETS DONE"[1]

At Nagesh's suggestion, and with his support, members of the newly formed GSS team visit some of the Energy Bridge teams to see how they work and gain some insights that will help them determine their own way of working. Doreen and Carl join them to learn more about how they could improve the way that the other teams at Reliable Energy share information.

What they see is that each team is a little different in what they share and how they communicate. Every team is completely open about where it stands with regard to what it is working on, what its immediate tactical (2-week) goal is, which intermediate (3-month) goals it is pursuing, and how those goals contribute to the strategic goal. Each of these goals is expressed in terms of the customer outcomes that the team is seeking to deliver, but other measures of team effectiveness that relate to their ability to reach these goals vary somewhat from team to team.

Carl, in particular, is concerned with this lack of standard reporting of measures across all teams. "How is management able to keep track of what the teams are doing? And how do they know when a team has gotten into difficulties and needs to take corrective action? Even in a world of servant leadership, surely managers need to know when they need to step in to help their teams? And how is senior management going to compare the performance of these teams?"

Nagesh responds, "We're concerned with the progress the teams are making toward their goals. Every two weeks we, and they, have an opportunity to see what progress they have made by looking at whether they achieved their tactical goal. We can also get some sense at that time of whether they are making progress toward their intermediate goal. Sometimes we all learn things that make us adjust their intermediate goal, including whether that intermediate goal is actually the right goal.

"We actually spend a lot of time during these biweekly reviews talking about goals and impediments, including things we can do to help them. We, as leaders, look for ways that we can help them to remove these roadblocks, and we look for feedback on whether our strategic goals are still relevant given the things that they have learned."

---

1. This is an old management truism, but in this case it tends to hold: People tend to do what they are measured on.

Carl's reaction shows that he finds Nagesh's answer a bit naive. "What about using measures like velocity and throughput that show how much work the team is producing? If units of work are standardized, you can compare the agile teams to other teams in the organization and gain insight into how productive and efficient the teams are. We've been doing that for some time and it helps to keep teams on track, and prevents them from wasting a lot of time and effort running 'experiments.'"

Nagesh responds, "We don't try to second-guess the team's approach. We don't monitor their 'productivity,' and we don't compare the 'performance' of teams. Every team is working on different challenges, and they need to have the flexibility to choose the best approach to meet those challenges. In our world, there are no 'standard units of work,' so we can't compare performance and productivity.

"That doesn't mean that we're not concerned about whether teams are struggling. If a team is consistently failing to meet its tactical goals, then we have a discussion with them about whether those goals were the right goals, and what they might do differently to better meet their goals in the future. We don't do this to punish them, but rather to understand whether we are all focused on the right things. Sometimes we find that they have been reticent to ask for help when they need it, or we find that something outside their control needs to be changed. But sometimes we do find that the team is not working effectively and we have to work with them to solve those problems."

MEASUREMENT CHALLENGES

Measurement is a contentious topic for most organizations. Managers want transparency into progress and risks, but too often the measures they impose on teams provide neither. Managers also discourage transparency when they use measures to reward or punish performance, causing employees to "game" the measures to make reality look better than it actually is.

We group measures into three broad categories[2]:

- Activities: Things that people in the organization do, such as perform work, go to meetings, have discussions, write code, create reports, attend conferences, and so forth.
- Outputs: Things that the organization produces, such as product releases (including features), reports, defect reports, product reviews, and so on.
- Outcomes: Desirable things that a *customer or user of a product* experiences. They represent some new or improved capability that the customer or user was not able to achieve before. Examples include being able to travel to a destination faster than before, or being able to earn or save more money than before. Outcomes can also be negative, as in the case where the value a customer or user experiences declines from previous experiences—for example, when a service they previously relied upon is no longer available.

Activities and outputs are easy to measure by simply counting things. Outcomes are much harder to measure because they require measuring the change in the customer's experience that results from using a product or service.

Shifting from focusing on activities and outputs to outcomes is especially hard in a siloed organization because hardly anyone actually interacts with customers. They view other departments as their "customers," which results in absolutely silly, even damaging, behavior. Other departments are not real customers, and acting as if they are makes it seem like satisfying the internal needs of the organization is more important than satisfying the needs of the actual customers.

Rather than tackling the hard problem of measuring customer outcomes, organizations often try to use activity and output measures as proxies for success. They may assume that a particular plan, if followed, will produce posi-

---

2. For more information on this, see the Evidence-Based Management Guide: www.scrum.org/resources/evidence-based-management-guide.

tive outcomes and, therefore, measure compliance with that plan in an effort to determine whether the project is successful. The reality is that all plans are bundles of guesses and hypotheses that, if followed, may or may not deliver anything useful. *On-time* and *on-budget* are poor proxies for success.

Not only are activity- and output-based goals poor proxies for success, but plan-based measurement is also demeaning and demotivating. When plans are devised by managers, rather than by the people who will do the work, they usually lack the hands-on experience and insights gained from actually working on the problem. Teams developing products and delivering services often have greater insights into what customers really need than managers who have only anecdotal experience.

> *Plans devised by managers usually lack hands-on experience and insights gained from actually working on the problem.*

Goals Are the Solution, and Sometimes the Problem

At the root of the problem is often confusion about goals and what constitutes progress toward goals. High-performing teams don't need to be given a plan, but they do need clear goals so that they can make their own decisions about what they need to do to achieve those goals.

Goals based on activities or outputs result in micromanagement just as surely as dictating a work plan to a team does.[3] When goals and measures are based on output, rather than on measures of the improved value that customers experience, work loses its "why."

Sometimes these goals focus on productivity, such as looking at how much work a team performs in a particular period. Productivity is only important

---

3. For more on this topic, see "OKRs: The Good, the Bad, and the Ugly": www.scrum.org/resources/blog/okrs-good-bad-and-ugly.

when the work being done by a team delivers some outcome that is valuable to customers. If you're still not sure about this, ask yourself which is better: going 100 kilometers per hour in the wrong direction, or 1 kilometer per hour in the right direction?

Effective goals are expressed in terms of customer outcomes, including the specific measures that express how the organization will know when the goal is achieved.[4] There are three types of goals: strategic, intermediate, and immediate tactical.

- A *strategic goal* is something important that the organization would like to achieve. This goal is so big and far away, and there are so many uncertainties that may be encountered during the journey, that the organization must use empiricism. Because the strategic goal is aspirational and the path to it is uncertain, the organization needs a series of practical targets.
- The achievement of *intermediate goals* indicates that the organization is on the path to its strategic goal. The path to the intermediate goal is often still somewhat uncertain, but not completely unknown, and is mapped out by a succession of immediate tactical goals.
- *Immediate tactical goals* are critical near-term objectives toward which a team or group of teams will work on their path to achieving the intermediate goals.

The relationships among these goals are depicted in Figure 3.1.

---

4. For a discussion of why S.M.A.R.T goals may not always be appropriate, see www.scrum.org/resources/blog/when-are-smart-goals-not-so-smart.

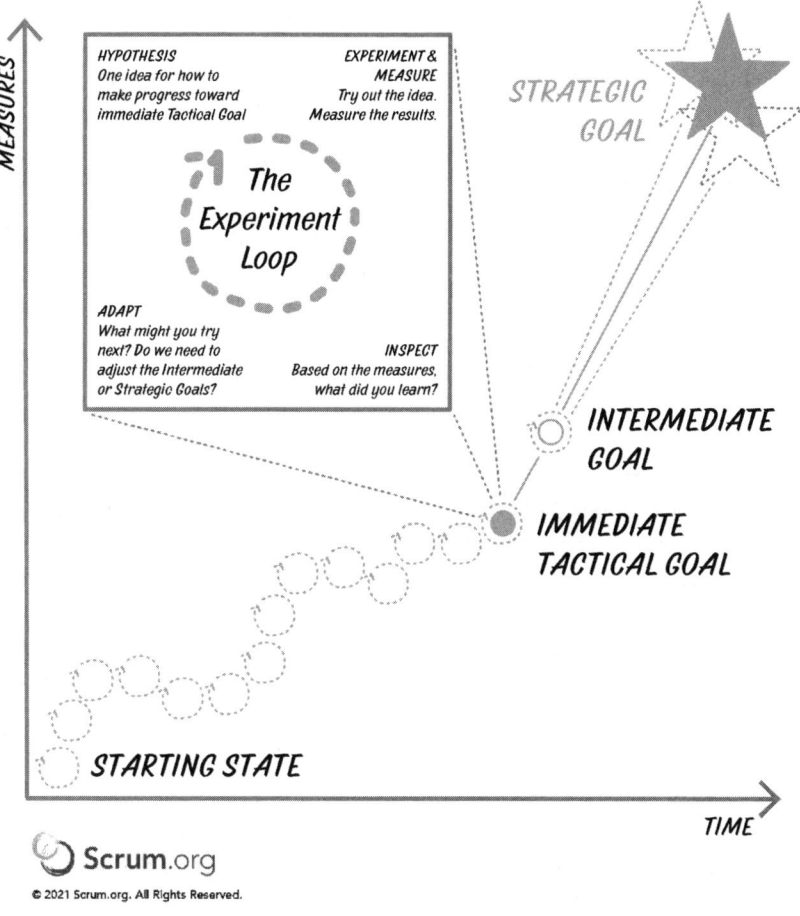

Figure 3.1 Reaching strategic goals requires experimenting, inspecting, and adapting[5]

In the context of the case study, the Energy Bridge teams have all three kinds of goals. At the beginning of each two-week work cycle (e.g., a Sprint in Scrum[6]), they form a new immediate tactical goal whose achievement, they believe, will bring them closer to their intermediate goal, and thus to the organization's strategic goal. Management can inspect their progress at any time, but especially at the end of the two-week work cycle (e.g., the Sprint

---

5. For more information on this, see the Evidence-Based Management Guide: www.scrum.org/resources/evidence-based-management-guide.

6. For more information on Scrum, see The Scrum Guide: https://scrumguides.org/.

Review in Scrum). Based on their accomplishments and learnings during these work periods, the team will adapt its work, and sometimes even its goals, to improve its progress toward the strategic goal.

Note that both intermediate and strategic goals may change a bit over time, based on things the teams and the organization learns. This does not mean that the team or organization "moves the goalpost" to make goal achievement easier; it does mean that goals themselves may need to be updated to reflect changes in customers' needs resulting from new customer insights from using the product/service, competitor offerings, or changes in the broader world.

LEADERSHIP, MEASUREMENT, AND ENGAGEMENT

> Carl is agitated by Nagesh's response. "It might work for a start-up to expect managers to engage in team-level reviews to find out what is going on, but that won't scale. Our managers are too busy to meet with teams for a half-day, every couple of weeks, just to make sure the teams are on track. We need dashboards or status reports that tell executives how the teams are performing. That way, when things go off-track, the execs can engage with the teams to help resolve whatever they are struggling with."
>
> Nagesh waits to see if Carl is finished. Then, when he is sure that Carl has finished venting, he responds: "I obviously don't know how your executives work yet, but at organizations where I have worked in the past, executives were spending time mostly meeting with each other, trying to make decisions with second- or third-hand information. They were making a lot of guesses based on partial information, and those guesses often turned out to be misinformed.
>
> "What we've learned, over time, is that teams have valuable information about customers, their needs, and what has been tried to meet those needs. That information can't be rolled up into a simple dashboard; too much nuanced information gets lost. We see our teams as vital engines of value creation for the organization.
>
> "The biweekly reviews of progress toward goals serve as vital forums for execs to understand what's happening first-hand. Our execs grew to appreciate those opportunities to really understand the business without layers of interpretation and filtering. They felt that it was time well spent, which helped them help the organization. Sometimes we even bring actual customers in for the biweekly reviews, and that has led to some very interesting insights that changed our entire strategy."

> Carl's agitation has increased and he is about to respond when Doreen interjects. "I'd like to understand better how this works, and I think we can try it with the new GSS team. I know that I have often felt frustrated that I didn't really understand what was going on, and I, too, have felt that our dashboards and status reports did not tell the whole story. I know that we've had lots of projects that looked great on the status reports until something blew up and we discovered that things hadn't been as rosy as the status reports were leading us to believe. Perhaps there is a better way ... ."

Each organizational layer that stands between executives and the teams who actually develop and deliver filters information, and often this information contains valuable insights or nuances that might inform different decisions. The middle layers often act with good intent, trying to respect the time of busy executives by reducing detail, but filtering requires subjective decisions about what is important and what is not, and it doesn't add value.

Unfortunately, this filtering is often driven by a desire, whether conscious or unconscious, to make things "look good." Each of the authors has witnessed well-meaning people arguing about whether a particular issue was "yellow or red" (somewhat concerning versus very concerning), with a bias toward playing down the severity of the issue because they didn't want to bear the brunt of executive ire.

This lack of transparency leads to the impression that things are going well, when the team may actually be struggling and needs to choose a different course of action. But when course changes are viewed as signs of poor performance rather than as positive adaptations to new information, teams tend to delay or deny those course corrections that are often necessary to produce positive results. Lack of transparency, over time, undermines the ability for the organization to make the decisions it needs to make to achieve its goals.

> *Lack of transparency undermines the ability to make decisions to achieve goals.*

It simply isn't true that busy executives don't have time to engage with teams. By engaging with teams and understanding their progress toward goals, including the issues that may be impeding this progress, executives become better able to help the teams as well as to inspect and adapt the goals for the organization. Strategic goals are not fixed in stone, but rather need to be continually adapted based on new information. Executives cannot get that information when it is filtered by false positivism.

An agile team responsible for delivering a set of outcomes to customers will take immediate action whenever they encounter a situation that prevents them from making progress. Such teams are typically not afraid to share information and make it accessible to everyone in the organization in open review sessions. With this behavior, there is no need for filtering information and leaders are needed only for ensuring alignment on goals, and supporting teams when they need help to solve a problem.

ORGANIZATIONAL CULTURE AND TRANSPARENCY

Transparency can seem threatening when organizations have become accustomed to false positivism, by which we mean that the organization's culture discourages people from saying anything but positive things about how things are going. While believing that dedication and perseverance can overcome most obstacles may have its benefits, only a reasoned consideration of all available information will result in good decisions.

When an organization is unaccustomed to transparency, new information can threaten the status quo. The following scenario, which is based on the authors' actual experience, illustrates the problem.

> The self-managing team decides they would like to understand the value they are delivering to customers. They instrument the features in the application to capture when that feature is actually used and for how long. As they review the data coming back from customers who are using the product, they discover that some of the features that they spent a lot of time developing are not being used very much, and some of them are not being used at all.
>
> When Carl, as head of the PMO, discovers this, he tries to direct the team to stop measuring the usage of features because he fears that it will make the stakeholders who argued strongly for the little-used and unused features, some of whom are influential executives, "look bad." He fears the criticism of those influential executives more than he fears having the teams build the wrong product.

For transparency to have a positive impact on the organization's ability to make decisions, the organization itself has to welcome it. The organization has to value improving its ability to deliver value over preserving the status of certain individuals.

Leaders have a responsibility to help the organization make this shift, by signaling the desired behaviors. To illustrate, consider the following true (but anonymized and simplified) story.

A new CEO holds a review meeting with all department heads to get their perspectives on their successes and challenges. In presentation after presentation, he hears what a great job each department is doing and how they are contributing to the success of the company.

At the end of the presentations, he thanks everyone for their efforts, but adds, "You know, last year we lost more than $100 million, our market value dropped by billions, and our competitors are making progress much faster than we are, so I know that everything can't be great. In future meetings, I'd like for you to share your challenges and concerns with each other, so we can help each other."

At the next executive review meeting, the first executive to present shares a much more realistic, even sobering, picture of how his organization is struggling with some key challenges. As he finishes, there is a moment of silence as everyone waits to see what will happen. Then the CEO does something powerful: He stands up and claps. He thanks the presenting executive for his candor, and he asks what help the executive needs from the CEO and the rest of the organization to start to overcome the challenges. He does the same with each successive presenter. It is just one meeting, but by this action the new CEO starts to build acceptance for transparency in the organization.

Trust is a necessary precondition for transparency. It takes a long time to build this trust and only a moment's ill-considered action to damage it. Leaders create the environment in which trust, and therefore transparency, can thrive. Since trust takes time to build, this creates a problem for newly formed teams: They have not yet delivered anything, so they have not yet earned the trust of the organization.

Lack of trust can create problems that actually impede the development of a team's ability to earn trust and reinforces the feeling that the team can't be trusted. An organization that doesn't trust its teams will make decisions about what a team is going to deliver and how they are going to work. By doing so, the organization limits the team's freedom to search out better solutions for themselves. This lack of empowerment often results in team members who are not engaged, but who would be engaged if they are not told how to work and what to build. Their motivation can be further affected when they lack the ability to choose who they work with and what they work on.

Helping teams to self-organize demonstrates trust, but it does not mean that team members are free to do whatever they want. Helping them to set meaningful goals, frequently inspecting their progress toward these goals, and then helping them to adapt their goals and their ways of working to better achieve their goals are important elements in building trust, fostering autonomy, and becoming high performing.

Once team members understand why their team exists, they can figure out how they will work together to achieve those goals, and what they are going to deliver to customers to help the customers achieve their goals. What they are going to build is actually the least important thing, because it will change over time. How the team works toward its goals, and the actual goals themselves, are far more important, because a team that gets those decisions right will figure out what it needs to deliver.

BALANCING INTERNAL AND EXTERNAL FOCUS OF GOALS OVER TIME

Carl is clearly skeptical. "Okay, I can see how periodic performance reviews, or whatever you call them, are a good thing. But how do you know if your teams are making progress without having plans with milestones and comparing their performance to those plans?"

Nagesh responds, "Everyone, from the teams to senior management, spends a lot of time asking ourselves whether we are headed in the right direction. So what we're concerned with is whether the team is, over time, reducing the *satisfaction gap* that we've talked about. We try to make sure that intermediate and strategic goals are expressed in terms of outcomes that, when delivered, reduce some group of customers' satisfaction gaps."

He continues, "Speed and productivity are important, but the problem with only looking at measures like speed and productivity is that you don't know if you're headed in the right direction. Speed and productivity need to be focused on delivering the right customer experiences. Once we're sure we are delivering the right outcomes to customers, we can focus on becoming faster and more efficient."

Strategic goals are best expressed in terms of achieving specific desired customer outcomes. Long-term value is only created by improving customer experiences and expanding the number of customers for whom the organization can deliver great experiences.

Intermediate goals are also usually best expressed in terms of customer outcomes, but sometimes the organization has to focus on other things in the short and medium term to improve its capability to deliver value.

Consider the case where an organization can deliver new capabilities to customers just once a year. At this rate of delivery, it will take a very long time to even measure customer experiences, let alone improve them. Clearly, focusing the short-term and intermediate goals on delivering faster will be important, until a frequent delivery cadence permits the organization to make frequent measurements of and improvements to the value the organization delivers to its customers.

Similarly, an organization might deliver value very frequently, but in very small increments because it spends a lot of time and effort fixing old problems or dealing with interruptions.

To get a better view of where an organization needs to improve, we use four different key value areas (KVAs) to help us consider where we should focus:

- **Unrealized Value:** The potential future value that could be realized if the product or service met the needs of all potential customers or users.
- **Current Value:** The value that the product or service delivers today.

The difference between the two is the *customer satisfaction gap*.

To consider internal capability, we consider two other KVAs:

- **Time-to-Market:** An indicator of the organization's ability to quickly deliver new capabilities, services, or products.
- **Ability to Innovate:** An indicator of the effectiveness of an organization in delivering new capabilities that might better meet customer needs.

Thus, an organization might deliver very quickly, but not very much in each release, if it spent too much time on non-value-added activities.

These KVAs are not measures themselves, but rather categories of measures. The specific measures will vary depending on the organization and its circumstances.[7]

GOALS AND MEASURES AT ALL LEVELS

> As a result of these discussions, Doreen starts to see that Reliable Energy's old mission statement, "Delivering reliable and sustainable energy products," was too high level to be a useful guide for making decisions. Moreover, it was internally focused, rather than being focused on customer needs. She can now see how teams might struggle to form their own tactical and intermediate goals.
>
> With Nagesh's help, Doreen leads a session with the agile teams to explore which outcome-based measures would make sense for the traditional Reliable Energy organization. Based on the work that the teams have been doing, they suggest further refining the list of customer types they had identified earlier (refer to Figure 2.2). They break down their customers into several groups—not just households and businesses, as they have done in the past, but into smaller, more refined subgroups such as electric vehicle owners, small power generators, and rate-sensitive manufacturers, to name a few.
>
> As their discussions proceed, they find that different groups have very different desired outcomes. For example, rate-sensitive manufacturers are willing to reduce their usage during periods of high demand by temporarily idling manufacturing lines to get a better rate, while homeowners who depend on Reliable Energy for heat and cooling are willing to pay a little more year-round to guarantee that their

---

7. For more information about these KVAs and examples of specific measures, see The Evidence-Based Management Guide: www.scrum.org/resources/evidence-based-management-guide.

power will not be interrupted when the temperature is above or below critical thresholds. And not everyone wants to generate energy; some customers do, but others simply want a reliable supply.

For each of these groups, they identify what they believe are satisfaction gaps, and they consider how their existing products and services could close those gaps. The team members also identify some gaps in their company's coverage, where the existing products and services don't address a satisfaction gap; they note that these are areas for potential future investment or acquisition.

The outputs from this session include a set of strategic goals, one for each product and/or service, with some initial thoughts on measures that would provide evidence that the strategic goal has been met. The big realization they come to as a group is that most of Reliable Energy's products and services don't measure customer satisfaction gaps as their primary measure; instead, they focus on internal measures such as revenue and profit. While these items are important, they provide little insight into where the organization can improve and where it can capitalize on new opportunities.

Most mission statements are vague and aspirational, suitable for publishing in annual reports but not specific or measurable enough to be useful in helping people and teams to guide their decisions. The technique just described here helps the organization to be more specific about *who* its customers are and what unmet needs they have. This, in turn, helps the organization form strategic goals that are specific and measurable, and that specificity helps the organization to be precise about its intermediate and tactical goals.

Sometimes, in applying this model, organizational members lose sight of who the organization seeks to benefit; they mistakenly focus on the satisfaction gaps of their executives, and not their customers. In a perfect world, of course, these satisfaction gaps would be aligned. In reality, there are all too many instances where executive needs for recognition or status drive behaviors that reflect little consideration of customer needs.

This is not to say that employees', including executives', happiness is unimportant: Customer satisfaction usually suffers when employees are unhappy. Strategic goals should focus on closing customer satisfaction gaps, but intermediate and tactical goals might focus on employee satisfaction gaps as necessary steps toward improving customer outcomes.

Customer satisfaction usually suffers when employees are unhappy.

All teams in the agile cell (GSS and Energy Bridge teams) take the strategic goals identified during the executive workshop and further refine them into intermediate and tactical goals (see Figure 3.2). As they consider the teams' goals, Doreen has an insight that she shares with Nagesh.

"I like the initiative and engagement that we're seeing from the teams. I can see how we will be able to have much more meaningful conversations about progress by looking at how each team is moving toward its goals. I also see something new that we, as leaders, will need to do. We need to look at whether, if every team were to achieve its goals, our company will achieve its strategic goal. If it won't, then there's something missing in our strategy."

Nagesh responds, "That's a really important insight. We now have more ways to think about strategy, and we have ways to continually test and improve that strategy as we get new information from the work the teams are doing."

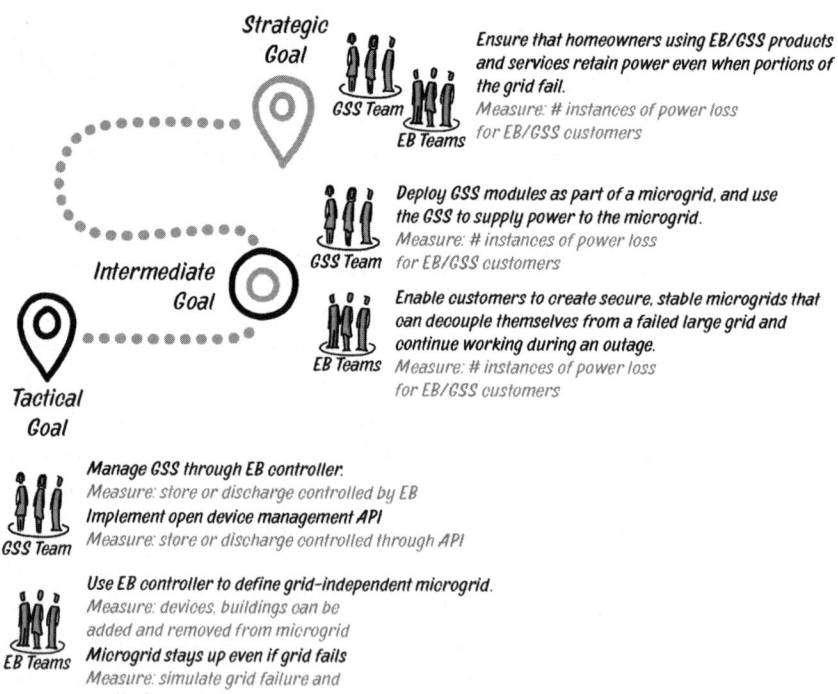

Figure 3.2 Example strategic, intermediate, and tactical goals

REFLECTIONS ON THE JOURNEY

PLAN-DRIVEN **GOALS** TO **GOAL-DRIVEN** **PLANNING**

STOP MICRO MANAGEMENT
Focus on outcome over output

- WORK WITH THE TEAMS
- INSPECT & ADAPT
- ASKING FOR HELP IS GOOD

TRUST

Strategic Goal

Set these as management

CUSTOMER OUTCOMES

Intermediate Goal

Collaborate on setting these

FEARLESS TRANSPARENCY

Tactical Goal

Let the teams set these

For agile teams to embrace their mission of closing customer satisfaction gaps, agile leaders need to let go of telling the teams what to do and how to work, or even reviewing and approving the team's plans for what it will do and how it will work. Instead, leaders must refocus their attention on the goals that they want to achieve and let the teams figure out how to achieve those goals.

This does not mean that agile teams lack accountability and oversight, but the focus of that accountability shifts from adhering to a plan to achieving important goals. Oversight focuses on inspecting the team's progress toward goals and helping the team members adapt their future path based on what they learn by delivering products or services to customers. Helping teams to adapt their course based on feedback requires absolute transparency, free from fear of criticism.

Achieving audacious strategic goals often takes a long time and many steps (and missteps) along the way. Intermediate goals can help both leaders and teams make measurable progress toward strategic goals by providing for ways to reach important steps along the way without having to wait until the end of the journey to know whether they are in the right place.

LEARNING TO LET GO

It's easy to think of an organization as a kind of machine for producing particular results, one whose roles, responsibilities, and processes define a kind of "work engine" that produces desired outputs. The reality is that organizations are complex social networks that reward people for getting things done. Compensation is one form of reward, but rarely the most important. Instead, the most important rewards usually relate to status: recognition, reputation, and influence. Introducing an agile way of working into an organization can change all three of these, often for the worse for the people who benefited from the old system. This is not a particularly new problem, nor was it new when Machiavelli observed:

> [T]here is nothing more difficult to take in hand, more perilous to conduct, or more uncertain in its success, than to take the lead in the introduction of a new order of things. Because the innovator has for enemies all those who have done well under the old conditions, and lukewarm defenders in those who may do well under the new. This coolness arises partly from fear of the opponents, who have the laws on their side, and partly from the incredulity of men, who do not readily believe in new things until they have had a long experience of them.[1]

---

1. Niccolò Machiavelli, *The Prince.*

This chapter explores how the agile leader helps the organization take its first steps toward empowering teams by letting go of old ways of working and the reward structures that enabled them, and by starting to build the reward structures that reinforce the new way of working.

EMPOWERMENT DOESN'T COME FOR FREE

With Nagesh's help, and aided by their collaboration with other teams in the agile cell, the GSS team has been making great progress in increasing their transparency and collaborating with their customers and other stakeholders. As they have improved their capabilities, they have discovered several improvements that they think will help them even more. The team has invited Doreen and Nagesh to join them in a retrospective to discuss their suggestions.

On the day before the retrospective, Nick, the head of engineering for Reliable Energy, approaches Doreen with concerns. "I've been hearing some complaints about the GSS team. While I wholly support exploring new ideas, we have an established channel for doing so: the Engineering Advisory Board. I've heard from our Chief Architect that the teams in the agile cell have been ignoring established technology standards and trying new things without approval. If we let every team do this, the result will be chaos. We can't let this go on."

Doreen listens attentively but pushes back gently. "Nick, I know that standards are important, but we've also discussed in our leadership team meetings that we need to try new things. And if I recall correctly, the Engineering Advisory Board meets only once a month. We need to let teams go faster; it will help all of us learn. And you know as well as I do that the best way to learn is to try to build something. We need to work with them, learn from them, and all our teams, so that we can adapt more quickly."

Nick clearly doesn't like Doreen's observation that his engineering organization can't make decisions quickly, but he doesn't have a good response. Doreen continues, "Let's talk with the teams to figure out where the lines can be drawn between what they can decide independently, what they have to comply with, and when we all need to work together to negotiate a new boundary."

An hour before the GSS team's retrospective, Ellen, the head of marketing for Reliable Energy, also approaches Doreen, obviously concerned. "I'm concerned about the messages that the teams in the agile cell are sending to customers," she starts. "It's come to my attention that they've been talking to customers, doing their own market research. My market research team is wondering why they aren't involved in this and, frankly, I am, too. We need to carefully control the messages we send to customers so we don't confuse them and lose them to other competitors."

Doreen responds, "Ellen, I'd love to talk about this right now, but I've got another meeting to go to. Can I come back to you on this?"

During their retrospective, Doreen listens attentively to the GSS team's suggestions, with the issues that Nick and Ellen raised foremost in her mind. She understands their concerns, but she also recognizes that Reliable Energy is going to have to work differently than it has in the past so that the organization can thrive in the future. As the meeting starts, she recognizes most of the team as long-time Reliable Energy employees who probably know the company's business and customers as well or better than she does.

The team proposes a number of interesting changes to the way that Reliable Energy currently operates. These changes include releasing very small improvements in product capability without going through the current, cumbersome integrated release process run by the Quality Assurance team in the Engineering department, and without having to clear the new features with the marketing department.

"These changes would help us to try new ideas quickly. Marketing wants to batch up the new features so they can do a big press release, and they think that customers can't absorb more than one release a year," one of the team members observes.

Another chimes in, "That might be true when releases are huge and complex, but we've heard from the customers in our early release program that they appreciate seeing constant small improvements in the product, especially when we are able to provide rapid and reliable security updates."

"There is actually something more important," one team member starts to say, and the other team members pause because they know what's coming. "We think we're making a lot of progress and discovering better ways of working, but we're increasingly getting pressure to revert to the 'the way things have always been done around here.' People say that they want agility, but when it starts to threaten the status quo, people push back. I think they'd prefer that we go back to being 'order-takers' and simply use agile as a way to 'deliver faster and more efficiently.'"

Agility isn't really about delivering faster and more efficiently. That happens as a by-product of improving ways of working to eliminate waste in both the process and the product, but the primary goal is to deliver better outcomes by obtaining frequent feedback, inspecting the results, and adapting based on that feedback. By starting to test assumptions early in the process, the team members will shorten their time to learn.[2]

The scenario described in the case study is quite common: Everyone loves agility until it starts to undermine their own perceived authority. This is especially true for executives who have been used to "calling the shots." They typically don't express their concerns as a loss of control, but rather focus on concerns about quality and consistency, whether in processes or messaging.

Everyone loves agility until it starts to undermine their own perceived authority.

Empowered teams are deeply threatening to traditional organizational hierarchies. When the traditional organization is threatened, it tries to constrain the change, limiting it to minor improvements in delivery processes. While the organization still realizes some benefits, it fails to achieve the motivational advantages that empowered teams provide, and it fails to significantly improve its ability to quickly respond to change because decisions take too long to navigate the siloed hierarchy.

To counter these drags on agility, senior leaders must do two things: They must support and protect the nascent agile teams from being dragged back into old ways of working, and they must change the power dynamic in the organization so that people, and especially other leaders, in the traditional organization improve their own perceived status by transferring some kinds of power to the agile teams. Chapter 1 introduced the term "agile cell" as a protection mechanism for nascent agile teams that creates a space where these new power dynamics can be installed with less resistance and more support and focus from leadership.

---

2. See this blog from Henrik Kniberg for more information on this topic: https://blog.crisp.se/2016/01/25/henrikkniberg/making-sense-of-mvp.

There is an art to doing this, but its essence is to elevate the importance of supportive, nurturing, and coaching behaviors both by example and by changing the organization's implicit—and sometimes even explicit—reward system. This change has to come from the very top, and it has to be consistent. Inconsistent support for empowered teams will tell everyone that the shift toward an agile organization is simply a facade, and a lack of support from the very top will tell everyone that the shift is not really strategic. All too many agile transformations fail because they have support only from middle managers, and not from senior executives.

A related part of this art is that agile leaders cannot devalue the contribution that every person in the organization makes, especially the people in the traditional organization. In the early stages of an agile transformation, most of the organization will not be working in an agile way. If a schism develops between the agile and traditional teams over their perceived importance to the organization, the traditional organization will find subtle ways to kill the agile initiative.

A solution to this problem is to show how everyone contributes to the goals of the organization, but in different ways. Not all parts of the organization actually need to be agile; in fact, there are many parts of an organization in which stability and incremental change are not only important, but essential. Agility is essential where large customer satisfaction gaps exist or where customer needs are changing rapidly. In contrast, where satisfaction gaps are small and needs are stable, stable processes often best meet customer needs.

This is not to say that even teams supporting very stable parts of the business cannot benefit from being empowered to improve their own way of working. Modern agile practices owe their success to the work of Deming and others, and to models like the Toyota Production System, which were focused on improving complicated but not constantly changing manufacturing processes. The point being made here is simply that different teams will take different paths toward their organization's goals, and that agile leaders need to create space for everyone to contribute.

AGILE LEADERS HELP TEAMS TO GROW THEIR ABILITY TO REACH AUDACIOUS GOALS

Doreen leaves the GSS team's retrospective feeling troubled and a little discouraged. She can see that the GSS team is trying to do the right things and that they have made great progress, but she also realizes that shifting to an agile approach will be a lot harder than she had anticipated.

As they walk from the meeting, she asks Nagesh, "Is this how these things normally go?" Nagesh responds, "Do you mean the push-back from the existing organization?" She nods. Nagesh continues, "Yes. People in traditional organizations see themselves as doing their best to meet the goals of the organization. When someone comes along and tells them, even implicitly, that they are doing things all wrong, they react negatively. No one likes being told they don't know what they are doing."

Doreen absorbs what Nagesh has said. "I can see that now. We're asking people to do something they've never done before, and to abandon ways of working that have helped them be successful in the past."

Nagesh nods, and adds, "There's something else. For managers, we're completely changing their focus. They've been used to being the 'final decider' about all sorts of things. Now we're saying, 'You don't do that anymore,' but we're not helping them learn what they *do* need to do."

As they walk past an empty conference room, Nagesh motions toward the door. "Can I show you something?" On a whiteboard, Nagesh starts to draw the following picture (see Figure 4.1).

"We tend to focus on things that are visible to us. When we think about our organizations, we tend to focus on things like processes and structure, or on people's behaviors, or on the things that people say and how they communicate. But like an iceberg whose mass is mostly invisible below the water line, these visible things are not the most important things. We see superficial details, but miss their underlying causes."

Nagesh pauses here to make sure Doreen is taking this all in. She nods and he continues. "When we are trying to change an organization, we need to pay attention to these invisible things. We often talk about how an organization's culture is the hardest thing to change, but that is influenced by things like the values and purpose felt by people in the organization, by their beliefs, by their fears and aspirations. To change the organization, we have to tap into those invisible forces and use them to create lasting change. If we ignore the invisible forces, they will continue to act as obstacles to the results we want to achieve."

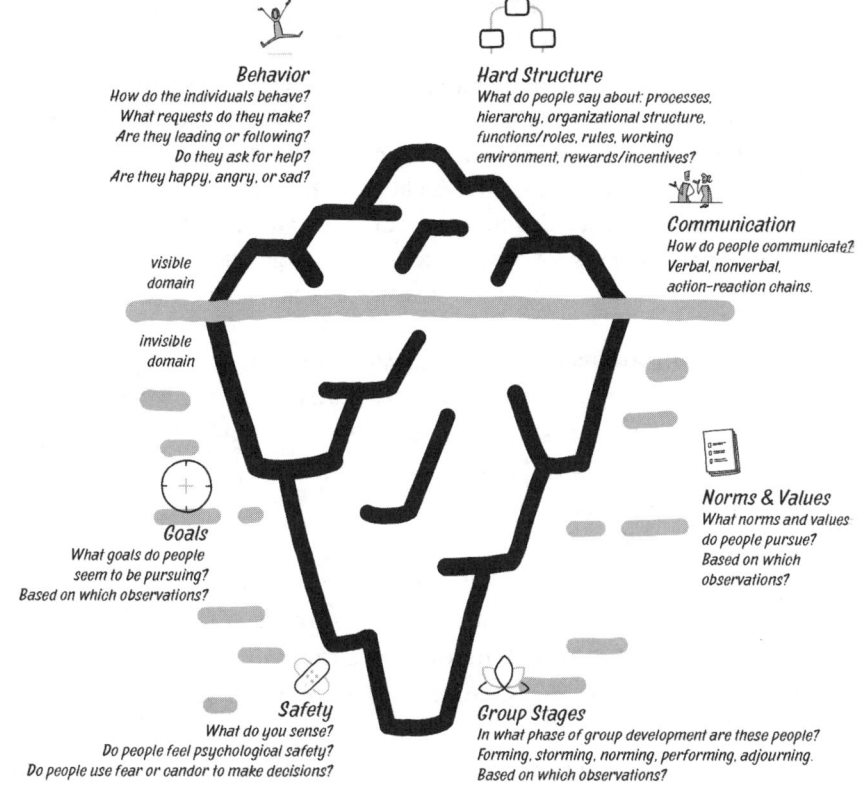

Behavior
How do the individuals behave?
What requests do they make?
Are they leading or following?
Do they ask for help?
Are they happy, angry, or sad?

Hard Structure
What do people say about: processes,
hierarchy, organizational structure,
functions/roles, rules, working
environment, rewards/incentives?

Communication
How do people communicate?
Verbal, nonverbal,
action-reaction chains.

visible domain

invisible domain

Norms & Values
What norms and values
do people pursue?
Based on which
observations?

Goals
What goals do people
seem to be pursuing?
Based on which observations?

Safety
What do you sense?
Do people feel psychological safety?
Do people use fear or candor to make decisions?

Group Stages
In what phase of group development are these people?
Forming, storming, norming, performing, adjourning.
Based on which observations?

Figure 4.1 Most leaders focus on the visible domain, but the invisible has greater influence.

Doreen seems a bit disheartened at all this. "Those things are incredibly hard to change. How can we possibly change all this?"

Nagesh continues, "When Energy Bridge was a start-up, everyone had the same goals and passion for what we were doing, and we all shared a common vision; the invisible domain took care of itself. As we grew, we mostly focused on the activities in the visible domain. Over time, we started to lose good people and we didn't know why. Then one day someone who had been with the company since the early days pulled me aside and said, 'People are leaving because they think that management is insensitive and disconnected. They feel talked-down to and disrespected. They feel like management isn't committed to the original goals of the company and are more concerned with their bonuses and status.'"

Nagesh continued, "This was a wake-up call. We finally figured out that we weren't investing in activities in the invisible domain. We started having regular sessions with the teams to explore how they could contribute to the mission, to the point where today everyone is involved in updating the mission as the teams learn new information. We learned the hard way that leaders need to balance their focus on the visible and invisible domains to help the organization to grow."

Most organizations focus on the visible domain. In fact, in the leadership training classes the authors conduct, nearly 80% of the participants indicate that they mostly focus on the visible domain. This same pattern plays out when one considers the stalled rate of agile adoption in recent years, and the reasons behind it (see Figure 4.2).

Organizations focus on the visible domain (processes, tools, structure, communication, key performance indicators) in the hope that doing so will lead to clarity and explicit outcomes. While these things are certainly important, excessive focus on the visible leads to employee disengagement.

Focusing on the invisible domain (alignment on values, turning values into a mission, coaching people in their personal development, and practicing by actively listening to people's problems and fears) helps to improve engagement and creates strong connections between people. However, only focusing on the invisible domain can lead to poor results, insufficient impact, and little customer value creation.

Balancing leadership's focus between both domains helps people feel engaged, helps them to continuously grow, and helps them to deliver better results for the organization and their customers.

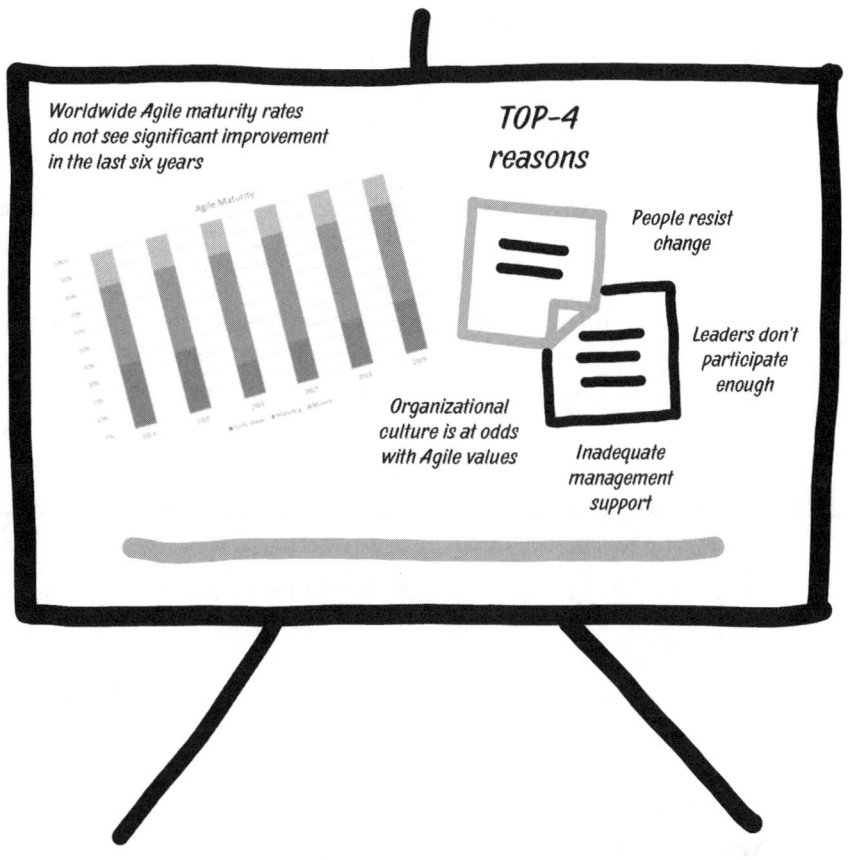

Figure 4.2 Agile adoption lags while common leadership problems remain unresolved.[3] (Source: VersionOne/digital.ai Annual State of Agile Report since 2014. Graph courtesy of Microsoft.)

ACHIEVING BALANCE BETWEEN THE VISIBLE AND INVISIBLE

Ensuring adequate focus on the visible domain requires attention to two aspects of communication (see Figure 4.3):

- Explicitness, which means establishing clear and measurable goals, and ensuring that everyone understands the goals well enough to start thinking about how they can contribute to achieving the goals.

---

3. For more information on the State of Agile Survey, see https://stateofagile.com.

- Presence, or one's ability to consciously choose a communication style and behavior that considers another person's needs in the invisible domain. Presence also means the ability to address and eliminate unwanted manifestations in the visible domain.

Measuring the *invisible domain* can be more challenging, but focuses on two related aspects:

- Ownership, or the degree to which a team is personally committed to reaching a goal. People who feel "ownership" experience intrinsic rewards whenever they make progress, however small, toward achieving a goal. As teams demonstrate greater ownership, they "earn" greater trust and often greater independence in self-managing. Granting greater freedom to these teams also sends a clear message about desired behaviors to teams that are exhibiting less ownership.

- Awareness, or the degree to which individuals are aware of their own motivations and the motivations of others in the invisible domain. Being aware of a person's driver in the invisible domain helps you to better cope with its manifestation in the visible domain. Explicit invisible drivers also help a team to discover their purpose and to recognize unwanted conflicting drivers. High levels of awareness tend to contribute to a person's appreciation of diverse perspectives because it helps teams to increase their creativity in solving complex issues. High levels of awareness also tend to increase a person's sense of psychological safety.

These aspects correspond with the factors that Google found in its research on team effectiveness:

- In the visible domain, teams create impact, structure, and clarity.
- In the invisible domain, teams have psychological safety, dependability, and meaning.

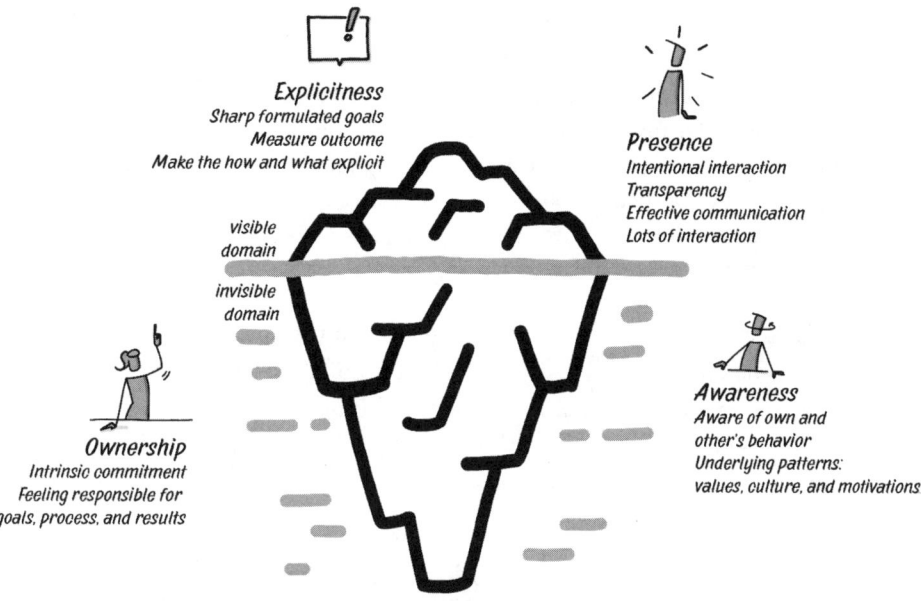

High-Performing Teams

Mature, professional, and engaged teams focus on the visible and invisible domains

Explicitness
Sharp formulated goals
Measure outcome
Make the how and what explicit

Presence
Intentional interaction
Transparency
Effective communication
Lots of interaction

visible domain

invisible domain

Ownership
Intrinsic commitment
Feeling responsible for
goals, process, and results

Awareness
Aware of own and
other's behavior
Underlying patterns:
values, culture, and motivations

Figure 4.3 Teams grow when leaders help them to focus on specific aspects.

LETTING GO IN SMALL STEPS

> At the biweekly leadership meeting, the progress of the teams in the agile cell has been a hot topic. "It certainly sounds like the teams have been busy," Carl observes, "but how do we know they are on track? Planning in 2-week cycles does not give us enough visibility into what they are doing, and what they plan to do, to hold them accountable. How do we know if they are going off in the wrong direction?"
>
> Nagesh looks around the room to see if anyone is going to answer Carl's question, but no one else seems to be rising to the challenge. "Carl, that's a good question. Let me answer it this way: If they had a detailed plan for the entire product release, how would we, or they, know that their plan was correct? If they didn't adhere to the plan, was the plan wrong, or is the team off-track? In short, we can't know."

"What we *can* do is to look at their tactical goals for their next increment and talk with them about how achieving those goals will contribute to our intermediate and strategic goals. If they don't achieve their tactical goals, we can talk with them about whether they need to adjust their approach or goals going forward."

Doreen jumps in, "The work these teams are doing is complex, with more unknowns than knowns. We simply don't know enough to make long-term plans."

Carl seems unsatisfied by this response. "This lack of planning simply seems to me to be bad management practice. We're putting a lot of trust in teams that haven't yet proven themselves. It might be okay for these few small teams to work this way, but the idea of expanding it to the rest of the organization makes me very uncomfortable."

For teams to grow, leaders must give them the space to grow. For teams to become empowered, leaders must let go of their own power and give it to teams. By doing so, leaders gain a different kind of power that comes from seeing the effectiveness of their organization, and their own influence, multiplied. But at the point where they make the decision to give away power, leaders make a leap of faith.

It's fairly easy to see where a leader falls on the trust–empowerment scale. You just have to look at what they manage (see Figure 4.4):

- **Activities.** Leaders who manage teams to perform a set of activities have very little trust in those teams, as in the case of traditional managers who use detailed project plans to track, manage, and monitor teams. Managing activities leaves very few choices to the team; their only freedom is in the small tasks that constitute the managed activity.

- **Outputs.** Leaders who manage teams to produce a set of outputs provide teams with the freedom to choose what they do, so long as they produce some set of outputs. Examples of outputs include product features, project contract deliverables, and various information reports. The teams experience a little more freedom than if they were managed to a set of activities, but they are still little more than "order-takers."

- **Outcomes**, specifically customer outcomes. Leaders who manage teams to produce a set of outcomes give those teams the freedom to not only choose what they do and how they work, but also what they produce to achieve the desired customer outcomes. Doing this demonstrates a very high level of trust between the leader and the team.

- **Societal impacts.** Leaders who focus on societal impacts are rare, and are most frequently seen in organizations focused on social causes or broader health and well-being initiatives, potentially spanning organizations. Leaders focused on societal impacts may have very little direct control over the work of their associated organizations, but can have tremendous influence on the success of their initiatives.

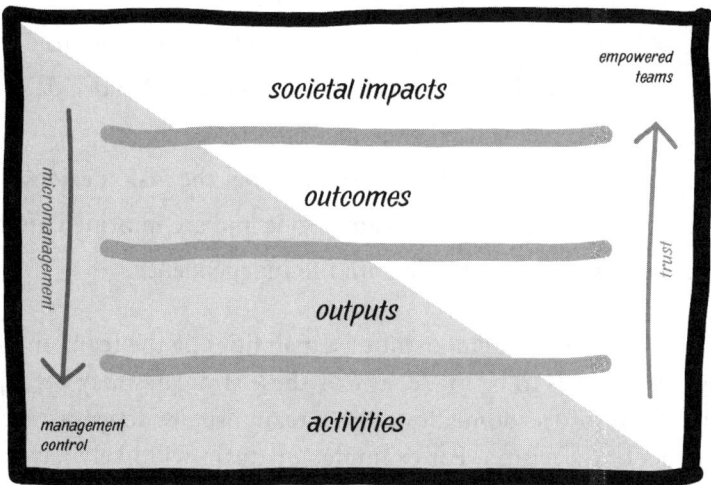

Figure 4.4 Stages of leadership focus.[4]

EMPOWERMENT STRATEGIES

In the preceding scenario, Carl feels very little trust toward the teams; he assumes that they don't know what they are doing unless they have a plan that tells them what to do, and his preferred management approach is to monitor the activities of the team to ensure they are performing to their plan.

---

4. For more information about empowered teams and agile maturity, see https://agileleadershipschool.nl/agile-maturity-model/.

This demonstrates a low level of trust and reflects a desire on his part to micromanage the teams.

Of course, leaders should not blindly trust teams to perform at high levels; teams need to prove that they are worthy of trust, and of the power to work independently that comes with that trust. Leaders and teams must negotiate an agreement about the appropriate level of trust and delegated power based on the team's demonstrated capabilities. This negotiation usually results in one of the following delegation strategies, listed from lowest to highest level of trust:

Seven Levels of Delegation[5]

1. **Tell:** Leaders tell the team what to do.
2. **Sell:** Leaders let the team try to convince them what to decide.
3. **Consult:** Leaders consult the team's opinion and decide.
4. **Agree:** Leaders and the team jointly decide.
5. **Advise:** Leaders share their opinion but the team decides.
6. **Inquire:** Leaders let the team decide and are informed after the fact.
7. **Delegate:** Teams decide with full independence.

Depending on the demonstrated capabilities of the team and the type of decision that needs to be made, any of these strategies may be appropriate, and the degree of freedom allowed to a team usually depends on the potential impact of a decision. For example, any team will likely have complete freedom to decide minor things like where to eat lunch, but only a few teams will have the freedom to set the overall product strategy.

Leaders have to decide which level of delegation is appropriate based on the maturity of the team and the potential consequences of the decision. Having a transparent conversation with a team about the level of independence for which they are ready can help the team to develop their decision-making capabilities. Leaders helping teams to develop greater autonomy can let the team make a minor decision, monitor the results, and then help them improve

---

5. Adapted from Management 3.0's delegation levels. For more information, see https://management30. com/empower-teams/delegation-empowerment/.

based on those results. As the team demonstrates sound judgment on small decisions, the leader can gradually expand their autonomy in making more impactful decisions.

Leaders have to decide which level of delegation is appropriate based on the maturity of the team.

SLOW DECISION-MAKING KILLS TEAM SELF-MANAGEMENT

It's not just who makes the decisions that matters, but how quickly those people make decisions. Waiting for people, resources, or decisions always creates waste; when a team has to wait, they will work on other things, but those other things may not be valuable. They may simply create waste that can sometimes take additional work to remove or correct. Waiting, in an agile system, is always bad. As evidence of this, the Standish Group's Jim Johnson reports in the 2018 Chaos Report that waiting for decisions—which the report calls "decision latency"—is a significant root cause of software project failures.[6]

An experience from the authors' own consulting work provides useful context. A product development team working for a telecommunications company was looking to improve the speed at which they were able to deliver new capabilities to their customers. They had a sense that implementing automated software build and test capabilities would speed their delivery.

As we worked with them to create a *value stream map* of their delivery process, we found a different problem: decision latency. The team was spending almost 70% of their cycle time[7] waiting for some other part of the organization to make a decision. Even automating 100% of their build test process would have saved them less than 10% of their cycle time.

---

6. For more information on the causes and effects of decision latency, see www.standishgroup.com/sample_research_files/BBB2017-Final-2.pdf.

7. Customer cycle time is defined as "The amount of time from when work starts on a release until the point where it is actually released. This measure helps reflect an organization's ability to reach its customer" (www.scrum.org/resources/evidence-based-management-guide).

This is not to say that automating build and test processes is not a valuable thing; it can be quite valuable, especially when it eliminates rework caused by human error. But it wasn't the largest source of this team's cycle time, and the same is true for most organizations. Communication delays, interruptions, multitasking, and decision latency are typically far greater sources of waste in most organizations.

WHEN YOU DISCOVER THAT YOU'RE THE BOTTLENECK, GET OUT OF THE WAY

The decision to let go of decision-making authority and transfer it to someone else, or to a team, can be frightening at first. In organizations in which decision-making power denotes status, giving up that power can seem like a resignation. At the point at which the leader confers power to others, there appears to be no guarantee that the leader will see any personal benefit from that action. Such a decision to give up power represents a leap of faith that it is the right thing to do, and that good things will come of it.

In reality, this decision represents an inflection point in the career of the agile leader: It signals that the leader is leaving behind reliance on formal authority and shifting toward indirect influence. Of the two, indirect influence represents a more powerful form of leadership because its span of influence extends far beyond the boundaries of formal authority. Developing the ability to influence others through example and inspiration allows leaders to tap into powerful motivating forces that order-givers will never experience. Teams that perform at the highest levels do so not because someone orders them to do so, but because in doing so they earn the respect and admiration of people whom they admire.

But for the leader just learning how to do this, it's a scary first step on a journey that may feel awkward for quite some time. The lack of a well-defined path with certain rules and prescribed outcomes is daunting, and when both the team and the nascent leader are new to having a dialogue about decision making, both are likely to make missteps at first. At these times, it is natural to want to retreat to old ways of working, but the better solution is to learn from the misstep and adapt, both for the leader and the team. By taking smaller steps, specific to the type of decision, and using the appropriate delegation level, it will become easier to let go. Doing so helps both the leader and the team to grow in their new relationship.

The reality is that traditional managers think they know more about how things should be done than they really do. When they start to trust their teams, they find that the teams, who are closer to both the customer and the work, are better able to decide how to work. When managers let go of feeling that they should have all the answers and embrace guiding their teams to find better answers, they find their influence and effectiveness are amplified, and they also free themselves to focus on seeking better goals rather than being stuck in merely seeking better means to reach goals.

DECISION LATENCY CAN BE CAUSED BY CROSS-TEAM DEPENDENCIES

Slow decisions can also result from one team waiting on another to do something, or waiting for an external expert with skills the team needs but does not have. Waiting for another team is sometimes caused by siloed skills, in which all the people with one set of skills that many teams need are located in one team, such as a database administration team or a security team.

Various solutions can help solve this problem:

- Improve the cross-functionality of teams so that they have the skills they need.
- Automate solutions so that teams can self-service.
- Break up the siloed team and assign them out to teams.
- Keep the siloed team structure but increase the number of people with the scarce skill so that no team ever need wait for help.
- Use a more hybrid approach of restructuring, with an emphasis on optimizing team interactions for flow.[8]

---

8. For more information, see the concept of travelers in the book *Team Topologies* by Matthew Skelton and Manuel Pais: https://teamtopologies.com/.

Organizations typically choose to use all these approaches in combination to reduce the decision/resource latency problem.

Decision latency can also be caused by a siloed product architecture in which each team owns a set of components. Teams developing new products or services that use these components often need to make changes to many different components. If the organization and the product architecture are siloed, that team will have to wait on many other teams to get their work done.

The solution to this problem is to eliminate the silos and let any team change any component, *so long as they don't break the component for other teams.* This last point is essential. Breaking the component for others can be detected and prevented by using automated testing, so that any deviation from agreed-upon behavior or performance (or security, reliability, usability, etc.) are detected anytime a team attempts to change a component. If any test fails, the change is rejected and prevented from affecting other teams. In fact, this approach is much more reliable than assigning the component to a team and expecting them to catch any damaging changes.

TEAMS CAN ALSO CAUSE THEIR OWN DECISION LATENCY

Even agile teams can fail to make timely decisions, such as when they continually postpone dealing with technical debt, or when they continually ignore problems identified in team retrospectives. Teams may fail to raise an issue with a stakeholder because they are afraid of being viewed as "troublesome." Or they may continue to develop new features without understanding whether what they have delivered to customers so far is valuable.

Agile teams can also experience group indecision. A team may feel that they need to reach consensus on everything and that anything other than unanimous agreement means they can't make a decision. While consensus is a wonderful thing, not everyone on a team is going to see things the same way all the time. Teams need to form working agreements that allow for moving ahead even when some team members disagree. This usually means they have to establish measures to test the decision (for example, by doing an experiment), and an agreement that these measures will guide any adjustments to the course of action.

Leaders can also help teams make better and faster decisions. They need to watch for signs of *decision procrastination* and help the team to move the decision ahead—not by taking over the decision, but rather by coaching the team to make better decisions on their own. This can be challenging for a leader who is used to making the decisions and to whom the decision seems clear, but if the leader undercuts the team's decision making, the team will never develop the ability to make their own decisions.

REFLECTIONS ON THE JOURNEY

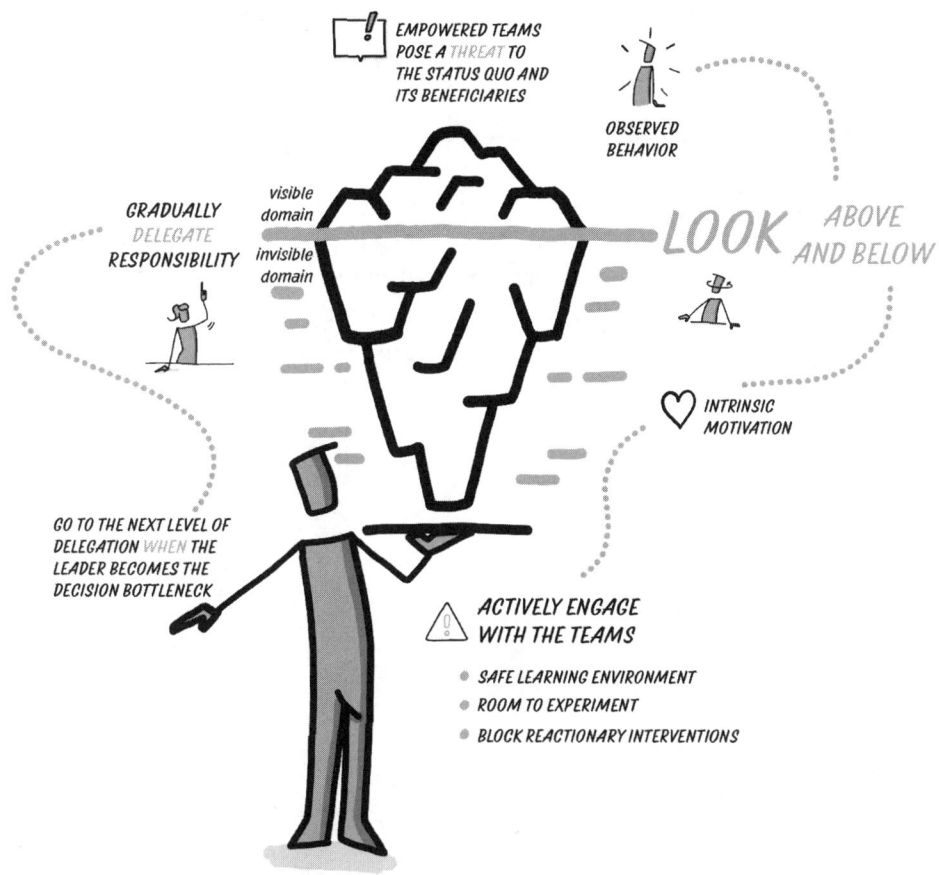

EMPOWERED TEAMS POSE A *THREAT* TO THE STATUS QUO AND ITS BENEFICIARIES

OBSERVED BEHAVIOR

GRADUALLY *DELEGATE* RESPONSIBILITY

visible domain

invisible domain

LOOK *ABOVE AND BELOW*

INTRINSIC MOTIVATION

GO TO THE NEXT LEVEL OF DELEGATION *WHEN* THE LEADER BECOMES THE DECISION BOTTLENECK

ACTIVELY ENGAGE WITH THE TEAMS

- SAFE LEARNING ENVIRONMENT
- ROOM TO EXPERIMENT
- BLOCK REACTIONARY INTERVENTIONS

Not everyone is going to like agility. More importantly, self-managing teams pose a threat to the parts of the existing hierarchy that benefit from that hierarchy because they will, eventually, reduce the scope and importance of the traditional parts of the organization. The people who benefit from the existing system are not naïve, and they are not going to accept a reduction of their scope and status without a fight.

Agile leaders play an important role in protecting self-managing agile teams from the potential harm that the existing organization might cause to them. Agile leaders need to both nurture those self-managing teams and gradually increase their empowerment by shifting responsibilities to the teams as they are ready to take them on, all while keeping the existing organization from preventing the self-managing teams from being starved of the skills and resources they need to grow.

Among the biggest change for both teams and leaders is accepting that not all experiments the teams run in pursuit of their goals will produce positive results. Traditional organizations that punish any shortfalls in results from expectations will kill agility. Protecting agile teams from this toxic culture is essential for creating an environment in which teams can try new things and learn from their experiments.

THE PREDICTABLE EXISTENTIAL CRISIS

Traditional organizations reward individual performance through a variety of mechanisms, including promotions, compensation, bonuses, and public recognition. These rewards can create a temporary sense of accomplishment in the minds of the people who receive them, and for some people they have a powerful effect on how those people perceive themselves. In the end, however, these kinds of rewards do not provide lasting motivation,[1] and they provide a false foundation for professional self-esteem.

Agile organizations also provide various rewards, but they tend to be focused on recognizing team performance rather than individual performance. Individuals on teams experience a sense of belonging and increased sense of self-worth through their participation as team members. While individuals can distinguish themselves through their individual contributions to the organization's purpose, the measure of their accomplishments relates to how they contribute to overall team performance, not on their individual results.

---

1. See www.danpink.com/books/drive/ and www.youtube.com/watch?v=y1SDV8nxypE for more information about Dan Pink's insights into motivation.

Not everyone likes this. Exceptional individual contributors who are motivated by a sense of being better than others may feel they have fewer opportunities to distinguish themselves. Their competitive behavior can actually interfere with their ability to be effective team contributors.

Self-managing teams also present a challenge for traditional managers of specialized functions within the organization by undercutting their authority to make certain kinds of decisions about career development, skill acquisition, or promotion. Once traditional managers figure out that self-managing teams need to take over significant chunks of the responsibilities that managers once held, they realize that their jobs, at least as currently defined, are at risk.

Agile leaders have two challenges: (1) to encourage self-managing teams to grow and thrive, and (2) to help people who have been successful in the old organization to find new ways to contribute, and if they cannot do so, to move them out of the organization in a way that is as compassionate and as disruption-free as possible.

In any organizational change, there will be winners and losers. To be successful, the agile leader must demonstrate that the new approach will work while protecting it from the old system that, although it may be failing in many respects, is still strong enough to protect itself when threatened with obsolescence.

NEW WAYS OF WORKING THREATEN THE OLD SYSTEM

Nick, the head of engineering, is waiting for Doreen when she arrives at her office in the morning. "I just wanted you to know that your *agile* experiment just cost us another one of our best developers."

Doreen senses frustration and hostility in Nick's voice. "What do you mean? Who's leaving?"

Nick continues, "Helmuth. I just found out this morning. He's leaving to be CTO of a start-up."

Doreen responds, "I'm sorry to hear that. But what does that have to do with our agile initiatives?"

"He said he doesn't see a future here, and he was concerned about getting his bonus. With teams taking on most of the technical decisions, he didn't like having to take on a coaching role. He said he wants to run big projects and make the key decisions. He can see where we are heading and he recognizes that he's not going to be in the driver's seat going forward."

Doreen takes a moment to understand what Nick is really saying. "Do you think it's a bad thing to have more people and more teams able to take on more complex technical work? I think it's a good thing to have knowledge spread more broadly across the organization."

"Yes, but we can't afford to lose great people."

"I think we want to grow more great people. If Helmuth feels threatened by the competition, maybe he's not as great as he thinks he is. We need leaders, even informal ones, who look for ways to coach others and help them grow, not hoard knowledge solely for their own benefit."

"But ..."

"Your point is taken, Nick, but what you're telling me about Helmuth is that he was interested only in his own success, not in helping everyone to achieve greater success. Maybe we're lucky that he's decided to move on."

But Nick isn't the only voice of dissent. Later that week, Doreen is cornered after a meeting with Marielle, the head of Human Resources.

"Doreen, can I have a word with you?" Doreen nods and listens. "I wanted to raise some concerns I've been hearing from a few of the leaders of our Centers of Excellence about the agile teams. They are all on board with helping people to develop skills, but they are starting to feel that we are sending mixed messages about career development."

"How is that?"

"Well, we're telling the agile team members that they should work together as a team and develop whatever skills they feel they need to meet their goals. But our career paths are aligned around the Centers of Excellence—development, quality, infrastructure, and business areas. Some of the members of agile teams have questioned whether those career paths make sense anymore. They feel it is more important to learn whatever they need to support their teams. If they do that, how are we going to help people to develop their careers if they aren't following our defined career paths?"

Doreen thinks about this for a moment. "It sounds like our career paths and maybe even our Centers of Excellence may need some rethinking. We want to encourage broader team member skills, but I also understand that we need technical depth to help team members to grow. Let's think about this. We want teams to be flexible, and maybe the CoE approach is too rigid."

Marielle seems frustrated. "We spent years rolling out these career paths, and employees have invested lots of time following them. Are we going to tell them that time was wasted? And what do we tell the CoE leads? They've bet their careers on this model. A few are starting to question whether we are really committed to technical excellence."

Doreen responds, "Wow! That's a lot to process. But, yes, we are committed to excellence, technical and otherwise. We're also trying some different ways to achieve that excellence. We've already seen a lot of benefit from encouraging teams to self-manage in developing the skills they need. I'm not going to tell them to stop; in fact, I love their enthusiasm and commitment to learning whatever they need to do to succeed."

Marielle counters, "One of the things we wanted when we set up the CoEs was to standardize skills across the organization. We felt that we needed to do that to make it easier to move people from one team to another. Now we seem to be undoing that. I don't recall that we made a formal decision to step away from that."

Doreen responds again, "We haven't made a formal decision, yet. But I wonder whether that goal to be able to move people around between teams was really a good one. We've learned it takes a long time for a team to come together, to reach high levels of trust and performance. We've also seen the motivational benefits of letting teams self-organize. And besides, I don't recall us moving people between teams very much because we haven't wanted to disrupt teams. There are other ways to improve the balance of skills across teams than the CoE 'silo' model."

Marielle is still frustrated. "I'm beginning to wonder what we're doing here. Everything about where we are headed runs counter to what we've been working on for years: standardizing career paths, standardizing skills, standardizing job descriptions. It's just anarchy."

Doreen responds, "It is a different approach. But I've never seen the kind of energy and engagement I'm seeing coming from our new teams. I'd like to see more of that. I can also see that we have a challenge with our ideas about career paths, and we may need to take a different approach. Let's get some time next week to talk about how we might learn from the experiments that we've been running to improve our approach to employee development."

> Marielle accepts that and says she will set something up. Privately, Doreen is feeling worn-down and a little beaten-up. She knew that building agile teams would be a challenge, but she didn't expect to have to fight her own organization so much. She is starting to wonder if the organization is really ready for the changes that are coming. And if it isn't, what does she do?

No one wants to believe that they are doing a bad job. For all the dysfunctions in traditional organizations—and there are many—these organizations are filled with people who think they are doing the right thing, or at least they are doing the best they can under often considerable constraints. The people in charge of the status quo are often very aware of the limitations of the current system, but they believe that the system can be improved incrementally.

When they are faced with a radical change, which they will define as some change that does not appear to involve them or the things they have been doing, they feel threatened. Their fears may manifest themselves in different ways, usually in the form of questions about the efficacy of the new approach, and if they cannot question that, then by showing that the new approach will undo important things that the organization has valued in the past.

Moving to an empirical approach centered on self-managing teams requires upgrading the "operating system" of the organization. The changes this brings threaten the organization in predictable ways:

- Changing the system to reward empowering others removes formal authority for decision making from managers and transfers it to the teams. This results in a loss of status for former decision makers.
- Replacing career paths with individual skill portfolios exposes the false veneer of certainty in career paths and promotability discussions, and replaces it with transparency about the inherent uncertainty of the whole concept of a career in a complex world.
- Replacing false certainty with true transparency exposes the false veneer of certainty of planning and predictability, and replaces it with empirical goal

seeking through experimentation and adaptation. In doing so, it can make the traditional management approach look willfully naive when it tries to enforce predictability on an inherently unpredictable world.

- Learning to trust bottom-up intelligence changes the role that managers have historically played in making the "big" decisions and being at the center of all activity. Agile leaders play an essential role in creating the conditions in which empowered self-managing teams can thrive, but once those teams are ready, agile leaders need to step back and let the teams achieve their full potential.

In short, embracing agility threatens much of the narrative that organizational members tell themselves about the foundations of their organization's success: that success depends on exceptional heroes who take charge, make critical decisions, and lead their organizations to win in a competitive environment. If this narrative sounds familiar, it should: It is the theme of myths and legends, and the classic stories of antiquity.

But what if those old myths are not true? What if success depends not on heroes and individual exceptionalism, but rather on heroic teamwork and collaboration? For an organization to embrace agility, it needs to create its own narrative and reject the cliches of the past. To see how organizations can do this, let's take a look at each of the changes noted earlier.

CHANGING THE SYSTEM TO REWARD EMPOWERING OTHERS

Traditional organizations reward people for their contributions in a variety of ways: through base compensation, through bonuses, through promotions to higher-status positions, through various kinds of public recognition that increase status, and through intrinsic rewards, such as letting them do work that they consider fun or enriching in some way. While monetary rewards are important, status and doing intrinsically enjoyable work tend to be more powerful motivators, and different people tend to respond differently to each of them.

Status tends to be the dominant motivator for people who ultimately seek management and leadership roles. Money is important, but as one goes higher in an organization and a society, even compensation is largely a marker for status.

To grow self-managing teams, someone must give them the power to make their own decisions. Managers who are motivated by status may feel that relinquishing decision-making authority means that they are losing status in this transfer of power. When they do, they may keep a tight grip on their decision-making authority and prevent teams from growing in their ability to self-manage.

Giving away power is more natural when a leader experiences an externally imposed transition, such as when a new leader joins an organization from the outside, or when a retired former star athlete makes the transition to coaching. In these cases, the leader has no established role or pattern of behavior and can choose to work in a new way.

> *Giving away power is more natural when a leader experiences an externally imposed transition.*

At these times of transition, leaders may more easily recognize that their success depends on the success of the people they lead, and that those people are closer to the real work than the leader is. In the words of Alex Ferguson, the legendary coach of Manchester United, "As hard as I worked on my own leadership skills, and as much as I tried to influence every aspect of United's success on the field, at kickoff on match day things moved beyond my control."[2]

What leaders in these situations discover is that one can actually gain respect and status by empowering others. Consider the case in which a child gains a greater sense of self-worth and purpose when an adult asks them to help them with a task. In showing trust and confidence in the child, the adult gains

---

2. For more perspective on this, see https://roneringa.com/leadership-lessons-sports-teams/.

greater respect and admiration from the child. At some level, everyone is still that child, and when an authority figure shows trust in them, they do everything in their power to prove that the trust was warranted. Wise leaders use this inclination to their advantage, so by appearing to give away their own status, they actually increase it.

Leaders have nearly endless opportunities to change the status recognition system in an organization, through public recognition and praise, and through promotions and other forms of extrinsic compensation. People are social creatures, and they are incredibly sensitive to subtle signals that leaders send about what is valuable and what is not. To shift the culture, agile leaders must start the change by altering the reward and recognition system that drives status within the organization, and they must be consistent in reinforcing the change over time.

The most impactful way for a leader to initiate such a change is to propagate the desired behavior by setting a good example—namely, by being willing to give others the recognition they deserve.

The conversations with Nick and Marielle triggered a deep desire in Doreen to understand why both are behaving in the way they are, and to figure out which values and beliefs are triggering their behavior. Since Nagesh came up with the iceberg model, Doreen seeks his help to understand the behavioral patterns of her management team and dive deeper into the invisible domain.

Nagesh reflects on some of his own experiences, "We had similar challenges at a critical point in Energy Bridge's early days. We had been founded by a couple of veteran venture capitalists who saw everything as a personal battle against impossible odds. They were exciting to work with, at first, but as we grew, the interruptions and emergencies they had to deal with made it impossible to work in teams. We lost a lot of good people before we figured out what I'm going to show you."

Nagesh walks over to the whiteboard and starts to draw a picture that evolves into Figure 5.1.

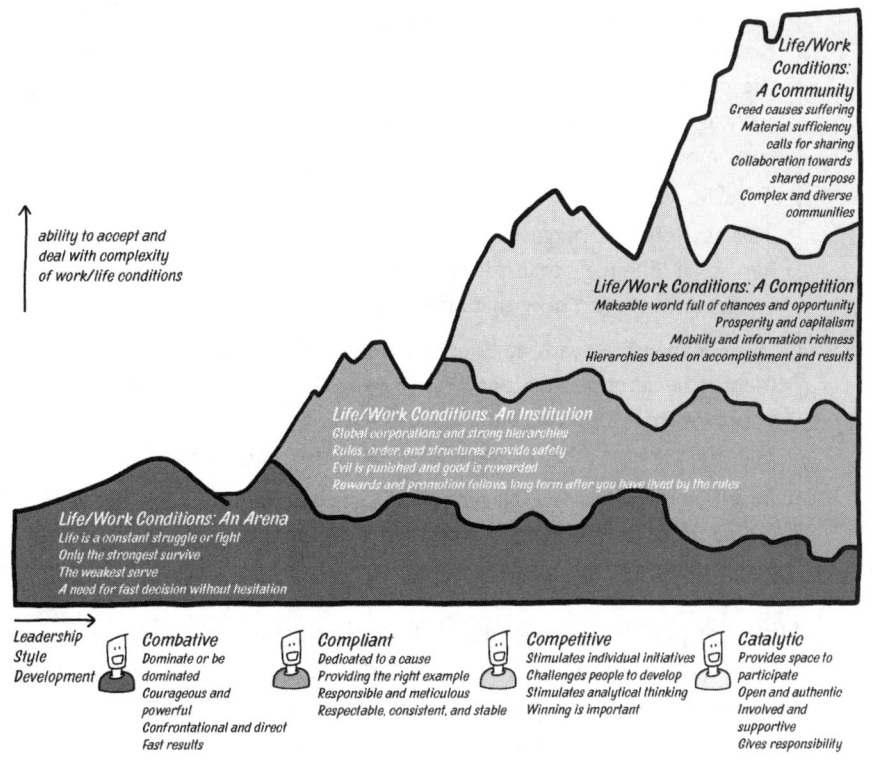

ability to accept and
deal with complexity
of work/life conditions

**Life/Work
Conditions:
A Community**
Greed causes suffering
Material sufficiency
calls for sharing
Collaboration towards
shared purpose
Complex and diverse
communities

Life/Work Conditions: A Competition
Makeable world full of chances and opportunity
Prosperity and capitalism
Mobility and information richness
Hierarchies based on accomplishment and results

Life/Work Conditions: An Institution
Global corporations and strong hierarchies
Rules, order, and structures provide safety
Evil is punished and good is rewarded
Rewards and promotion follows long term after you have lived by the rules

Life/Work Conditions: An Arena
Life is a constant struggle or fight
Only the strongest survive
The weakest serve
A need for fast decision without hesitation

Leadership
Style
Development

Combative
Dominate or be
dominated
Courageous and
powerful
Confrontational and direct
Fast results

Compliant
Dedicated to a cause
Providing the right example
Responsible and meticulous
Respectable, consistent, and stable

Competitive
Stimulates individual initiatives
Challenges people to develop
Stimulates analytical thinking
Winning is important

Catalytic
Provides space to
participate
Open and authentic
Involved and
supportive
Gives responsibility

Figure 5.1 Different leadership styles have differing ability to deal with complexity.

"This model," Nagesh explains, "reflects how we typically adapt our leadership style to deal with more complexity in our environment. The typical leadership styles that we often see in organizations are the combative, compliant, and competitive styles. Just have a look at the reward systems we use at Reliable Energy and you will find lots of similarities."

Nagesh continues: "What we had to learn the hard way at Energy Bridge is that these three leadership styles were no longer suitable to fix the issues associated with the market conditions we were experiencing. What we are trying to do with this agile way of working is to create a culture in which we can tap into the collective knowledge of our people, so we can come up with smarter decisions faster. To do this we need a leadership style that stimulates people and teams to make more decisions. We called this the 'catalytic leader.'"

"The new breakthroughs and challenges of this complex digital age are inherently creating some challenges that require us to build organizations that can tap into the collective intelligence of multidisciplinary teams. The only way to develop a truly agile culture is to gradually shift our leadership style toward one that stimulates more team ownership, collective knowledge, and goal/value-driven decision making."

This session with Nagesh has been one of Doreen's most valuable moments with him so far. She feels that it is finally becoming clear why people sometimes behave in certain ways and how that affects others.

"Our leadership team at Energy Bridge made a huge step forward at the moment it became transparent what cultural issues and individual norms and values people were using," Nagesh mentions. "And as it turned out, a lot of the leadership behaviors were related to how we were rewarding people."

Based on these insights, Nagesh and Doreen agreed to share this model among the members of the management team in an open conversation.

Different people will respond differently to this shift in reinforcements and rewards, depending on the way that they respond to increasing complexity. As the model shown in Figure 5.1 illustrates, there are many kinds of people who will benefit from keeping the system the way that it is.

The journey toward a catalytic leadership style can be difficult and the road full of obstacles. The further one's current leadership style is from this catalytic style, the harder it gets and the longer it takes:

- Leaders who still use a combative leadership style, fighting to gain or retain power, first need to experience how it is to share their power through a system of rules that provide security and safety. Jumping right to a catalytic style is not sustainable, since they never really get the opportunity to feel and understand how to handle the two value systems in between.

- Leaders with a compliant style first need to experience how they fulfill their individual needs within a system that has rules and opportunities, since they are used to the idea that individualism is often perceived as breaking the institution's rules.

- Only in a healthy, competitive culture can you start experimenting with a leadership style that gradually transfers to teams (using the delegation levels mentioned earlier).

Combative Leadership Style

Leaders with a *combative* leadership style are strong individuals who continually fight against forces that prevent lesser people from achieving great things. They are the people who, despite overwhelming odds, nearly single-handedly saved the company, or a product, or a project, from near-certain ruin. They promote a narrative that the organization is in a constant battle for survival, and that only their strong, decisive, and even combative leadership style is staving off certain disaster.

The problem with combative leaders is that they are the stars of their own narrative, and everything revolves around them; they're focused on their own success, and if the rest of the organization also succeeds, that's purely an accident of chance. Organizations that rely on combative leaders to save them are forever careening from one crisis to another, forever in need of their leader to save them because they never develop the everyday skills necessary to deal with complexity. Their reliance on combative behaviors keeps them trapped in perpetual crises—crises that are sometimes actually created by these leaders themselves.

Compliant Leadership Style

Mature organizations in relatively uncompetitive environments often exhibit the *compliant* model of leadership, in which long-standing leaders preside over a stable hierarchy that rewards and protects the status quo. The main role of these leaders is to prevent change from upsetting a system that they believe works quite well as it is. Organizations that are required to project stability and trustworthiness often have compliant leadership—for example, banks and insurance companies, law and accounting firms, public utilities, and government agencies. Alternatively they may be privately held, long-standing companies in noncompetitive markets that are owned by a single family or family group.

Compliant leaders, in seeking to minimize change, cripple their organization's ability to respond to change. Their simple narratives about what is acceptable behavior and what is not acceptable do not allow for challenging the accepted dogma. As a result, they spend their energy resisting change instead of harnessing it as a creative force. The leaders themselves embrace the entitlement and privilege of a "ruling class," and the leadership teams can seem almost like an exclusive social club. Compliant leaders can be very patriarchally supportive of their employees, provided that those subordinates are compliant and adhere to unwritten but recognized protocols, and so long as the decisions of the leaders are not questioned.

Competitive Leadership Style

Organizations with a *competitive* leadership style are much more tolerant of change because change provides opportunities for people to distinguish themselves from their peers. People in these organizations tend to view the world in competitive terms, as competition provides the means by which leaders "rise to the top" and by which employees prove themselves capable. Competitive organizations are intensely individualistic, and a common management tool is stack-ranking employees by performance.

The main feature of organizations where the competitive leadership style is dominant is that the members believe that the organization's leaders are in their roles because they are the best suited to lead; the leaders have earned the right to lead by their past performance. If that performance lags, the people in the organization accept that it is appropriate for new leaders to take their place. Examples of organizations that tend to have competitive leadership styles include venture capital firms and start-ups.

Because competitive leaders are in a competition with other competitive leaders, they can be blind to changes in the world around them. They tend to be internally focused on advancing their own interests relative to their internal competition. They can use external events to advance their own positions, but any improvements in the customer experience are mostly a secondary effect of the internal competition. This lack of external customer focus, and the leaders' lack of focus on helping the organization grow to meet new challenges, ultimately limits the ability of competitive leaders to create great organizations.

Catalytic Leadership Style

What differentiates the *catalytic* leadership style from the other styles (as illustrated in Figure 5.2) is that it seeks to help others develop their own leadership abilities. It does not look at leadership as the focal point for wielding personal power, but rather as a quality that anyone in the organization can exhibit when opportunities to do so arise

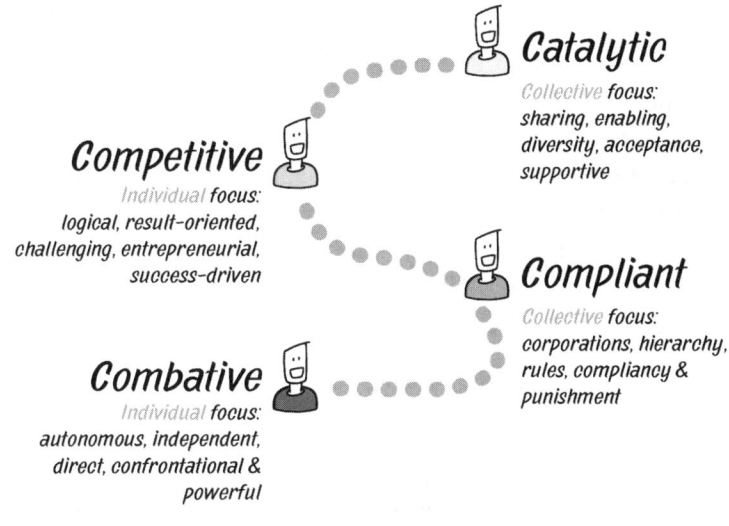

Figure 5.2 The catalytic leadership style has a strong collective focus.

Leaders who embody the catalytic leadership style seek to empower people in the organization so as to achieve greater results; as catalysts, they help remove barriers that are preventing the organization from being more effective. Catalytic leaders do this by helping people in the organization to grow, both professionally and personally, so that they are better able to work together to achieve goals that none of them, as individuals, could achieve. Like a catalyst in a chemical reaction that reduces the activation energy required for the reaction to start, the catalytic leader makes it easier for people to come together and get things done.

Cultural Leadership Styles and Agility

From the descriptions of these different cultures, it should become apparent that self-managing teams will thrive only under the catalytic leadership style. Self-managing teams are ultimately suffocated by the change-resistance of compliant leadership styles, and they are torn apart by combative and competitive leadership styles that value individual achievement over everything else.

Self-managing teams will thrive only under the catalytic leadership style.

Leaders who find themselves wanting to change their organization's dominant leadership style to support a catalytic leadership style need to consider where their organizations are today. All organizations have a dominant leadership style that is usually signaled by the leaders at the top of the organization.

Leaders in an organization with a predominantly combative leadership style will find it nearly impossible to change the culture of the organization toward a catalytic style of leadership, though they may be able to transition to a compliant style. In such an organization, there will be too many people, usually at high levels, who benefit from the perpetual cycle of crisis heroism that permeates the organization and who will oppose a culture change. Combative leadership is toxic to the self-managing team.

Leaders in organizations with a predominantly compliant leadership style might see that their organization needs to change to be more effective at dealing with change. They might think that they can dictate the way that the organization looks at leadership, principally by establishing rules about how the organization will work in an agile way, rules to which everyone must adhere. As long as they are leading the change initiative, the organization will appear to be changing. Unfortunately, as soon as they step away, the organization will go back to working in the old way since the very stability that the organization craves will stand in the way of real change. The culture change may be tolerated in pockets such as innovation labs, but it will never really affect the mainstream organization.

Leaders in organizations with a competitive leadership style have a better chance of changing, provided that leaders can demonstrate that a catalytic leadership culture produces inherently better results. Leaders in combative and compliant cultures may have a better chance at moving their organization to a catalytic culture if they first move the organization to a competitive leadership culture (see Figure 5.1), which may be more accepting of a further evolution.[3]

REPLACING CAREER PATHS WITH INDIVIDUAL SKILL PORTFOLIOS

Traditional organizations use career paths to reinforce their existing structure. The career paths represent a formal articulation of how people are expected to progress in the organization, saying, in a sense, "If you do the following things, you will be rewarded." However, a carved-in-stone career path creates a false sense of certainty in a world that is uncertain and complex.

In the case study, the head of the human resources department expresses concern over the challenge that self-management represents to the idea of a career path. Likewise, managers in functional areas may promote the concept of a career path because keeping people in functional silos in the organization is the source of their own status and authority.

In modern organizations, teams are the fundamental engine for creating value. A lone individual, no matter how high performing, has very little effect on (or can even damage) the organization's ability to deliver value until they become effective members of a team.

For a self-managing team to thrive and grow, its team members need to grow their own skills in whatever way best fits their team's needs and their own personal abilities and interests. Each individual team member will, over time, develop a unique set of skills that helps them best perform in their particular team. Because every team's needs are different, every team's composition of people and skills will look a little different.

---

3. More information on developing a catalytic leadership style can be found here: https:// evolutionaryleadership.nl/leadership/catalytic-leadership-style/.

This is a nightmare for the traditional manager, who is primarily concerned with the interchangeability of people across teams, but it results in individual teams that are uniquely attuned to meeting the challenges they face. The "flexibility" that some managers want, so that they can move people between teams, is based on the false assumption that "bringing people to the work" achieves better results than "bringing work to the team." They have a flawed belief that people are interchangeable and that teams are easy to form. What these managers fail to understand is that high-performing teams take a lot of time and investment to create, and they are very fragile to changes in team members. Adding a new team member can throw a high-performing team back into the "forming" stage. Losing a team member can do the same.[4]

As organizations make the shift toward self-managing teams, siloed career paths become an impediment to growth; they reflect skills and promotional models that no longer reflect the direction in which the organization is heading. The idea of a career path itself is an outdated relic of an organization that no longer really exists by the time the organization really needs agility. Not only are the skills they encourage out of step with the skills demanded on agile teams, but the promotional paths that they promise no longer exist.

Members of self-managing teams will, through the course of their daily work, continually find new opportunities to learn new skills that help them contribute to new teams. Each team's needs will be a little different, and the skills that team members need to develop will vary in tandem. Although a new, basic set of skills might be required to lead an agile organization, no common career path could capture the rich variations in these needs; each team member needs to work out for themselves what makes sense for their teams and for themselves.

Individual skill portfolios reflect much better how individuals grow than common career paths do.

---

4. For more on how to help teams adapt to change dynamically over time, see Heidi Helfand's book *Dynamic Reteaming* (www.heidihelfand.com/dynamic-reteaming/).

Rather than thinking of taking steps on a fixed career path, today's team members are better served by thinking of their skills like an investment portfolio: one with some skills that are high performing today but may lose their value in the future, and with some skills that are not as highly valued today but may become more valuable in the future.

In a changing world, not all the problems that are apparent today will exist tomorrow. Skills that are useful today may be rendered valueless by shifts in the market and changes in technology. To protect against this risk, do what investment fund managers do: diversify. Having a variety of skills gives team members flexibility in the face of change.[5] To take charge of their own development, team members can work in a way that mirrors the way that fund managers balance the investments in their portfolio: They continuously identify underperforming assets and trade them out for assets they believe will perform better in the future.

Team members who think of skills in this way will find that they have some skills that are currently performing well but whose value may potentially decline over time. They will have other skills that they are just now developing but that will potentially become their most important skills in future years. Since they can't predict what those will be, team members will want to have a few skills that they are looking for ways to grow.

Over time, to make room for new skills, team members will have to let some go. If these skills are still in demand, they might seek to mentor others to take on the skills while they focus on newer skills. Or they might seek out people who are in a similar situation—people who are experts in one skill but who want to try something new. Which skills a person develops will vary based on that individual's personal interest and the needs of their team, and not on a rigid and externally defined career path.

Team members who have a number of things at which they are skilled are more resilient when the unexpected "skills market" correction happens, or

---

5. www.forbes.com/sites/adigaskell/2019/03/22/3-reasons-why-being-a-polymath-is-key-in-the-future-of-work/?sh=794a6ad06d38.

when new and unforeseen opportunities ("problems") present themselves. And in the process of developing these skills, team members acquire the most important skill of all: the ability to learn new skills.

REPLACING FALSE CERTAINTY WITH TRUE TRANSPARENCY

Many leaders say they welcome transparency and are open to change, but when confronted with uncomfortable facts their actions tell a different story: They blame the messenger, or they bury information that does not present an upbeat, positive spin on the situation. In truth, many leaders feel uncomfortable with transparency because it belies the "can do" attitude that they believe leaders must project.

Two examples from the authors' consulting experiences illustrate the point:

- Many teams with whom we have worked have been expected to prepare presentations for executives that recounted project status; presented progress, risks, and issues; and stated what was being done about them. The prep work for these meetings was substantial, and a fair amount of effort was spent trying to "spin" the status to make it look better than it was, so as not to attract unwanted management attention.

- Another team with whom we worked was doing an evaluation of a packaged application to determine whether it could be adapted to their needs. The team used an agile approach to actually adapt the package to meet a small but important subset of the real-world scenarios that they would need to handle. After a month of effort, they succeeded in adapting the package to meet these needs, but also discovered that adapting it to meet all the organization's needs would be prohibitively expensive. The project was canceled, saving tens of millions of dollars and years of effort, but some managers still considered it a failure because the team had not produced a workable solution for the amount the organization could afford to spend.

Many organizations put such a premium on "predictability" that anything that does not deliver the wished-for results is considered a failure.[6] As a result, people feel pressure to tell leaders what they want to hear, not what they need to know; they "spin" information to make it look more positive, and they hide information that they cannot spin. As a result, leaders continue to be surprised by bad news that they would have preferred to know earlier.

The solution is, at least conceptually, easy: Encourage—even demand—full transparency. One of the authors had a manager who used the expression "Facts are friendly"; this is a valuable outlook. In a sense, all news is good when it provides an accurate picture of where you are; "bad news" can be even better than "good news" because it tells you that you need to do something different. If your preconceptions are always validated, you will never learn anything.

Putting this into practice is harder, especially in organizations that are not used to full transparency. When an organization is unaccustomed to transparency, leaders know that information is filtered and "spun," which tends to amplify the magnitude of "bad news" when it finally wriggles its way into view. In other words, because most information is filtered in such an organization, any bad news that leaders get must be *really* bad. When the organization starts down the path toward full transparency, leaders need to make a conscious effort to intercept this response and consider the information dispassionately. Repeating "Facts are friendly" as a mantra helps to counter emotional responses to "bad news." In a culture that embraces transparency, there is no such thing as "bad news"; there is just "news."

An organization that has become accustomed to a steady diet of rosy-colored, upbeat information needs a bit more help. Leaders need to recognize and thank people for their transparency, and to stop rewarding people for putting a positive spin on untoward news. When leaders detect that they are not getting the full truth, they need to keep digging until they are satisfied that they have the whole story. Leaders need to become, in some respects, detectives who seek transparency.

---

6. For more on this topic, see www.scrum.org/resources/blog/escaping-predictability-trap.

Leaders need to become transparency-detectives.

Sometimes "the truth" is not clear-cut or conclusive; there may not be clear answers to some questions. "I don't know" has to be an acceptable answer, if it is an honest statement. Leaders can encourage transparency by accepting that some questions don't yet have answers, and they can help teams to achieve better results by going further, by saying, "It's okay that we don't know that yet, but what can we do to learn more, together?"

LEARNING TO TRUST BOTTOM-UP INTELLIGENCE

On December 15, a massive cold front moves into the area. As temperatures plummet by more than 20 degrees below normal for that time of year, the demand for power dramatically spikes. Aging power transmission substations, not adequately conditioned for the cold, fail, as do stand-by generators that had not been adequately tested. Power demand starts outstripping the supply, and the resulting imbalance causes a further cascade of failures in the national grid. Late in the day, a short at a major transmission substation knocks out power to more than 2 million customers. The bill for years of under-investment in the national power grid is about to come due.

Even though these failures are mostly happening outside Reliable Energy's distribution network, the company is hardly unaffected. The operations management center begins to see the effects of the failing grid through the afternoon. Even though those issues aren't under their control, the problems elsewhere on the grid are starting to affect Reliable Energy's customers. Doreen gets the call just after 9 pm, and she reaches out to all her managers to convene a call to decide what to do.

Nick, the head of engineering, is adamant: "We need to shut down our sub-grid immediately. If we don't, as demand outstrips supply in the rest of the grid, it could damage our transmission equipment."

Julie, the head of Public Relations, jumps in: "I understand that, but if we do, angry customers will find a way to blame us. We can't have this look like our fault."

Doreen, who understands the risks that both Nick and Julie are pointing out, asks, "How long will it take us to put a workaround in place? Don't we have contingency plans for this?"

Nick replies, "We have plans for what to do if our sub-grid fails, but we always assumed that the national grid would have its own plans for dealing with its part. Obviously, those plans haven't worked. We need to shut down our grid now, if we want to avoid major damage to our network."

Doreen scowls, "Customers depend on us for heating their homes. If we shut off power in this kind of weather, we're affecting people's lives. We need a better answer."

Nick responds, "It's late in the evening and I've got calls out to my managers. We're going to have some calls tonight to develop a plan, and we should be able to have something to discuss first thing in the morning. In the meantime, we need to shut down our grid."

Nagesh has joined the call at some point during the preceding discussion and now jumps in. "Sorry I'm late; I've been on the phone with our teams who have been working with the Network Operations Center (NOC) teams all afternoon. They think they have a solution and have been carefully trying some things that seem to be working. They don't think we'll need to shut down our grid."

Nick is clearly surprised by this news, and just as clearly annoyed, "Whatever it is that they've been doing, it's not been cleared through the engineering management chain. We need time to review their proposal."

Doreen and Julie, though, are cautiously elated. Doreen asks, "That's great news! What's their solution?"

Nagesh continues, "You probably know that we've been working with the NOC to test the interface with the national grid. Our testing has been going well, and the NOC and product teams have been working together all day to gradually transfer network management control to the new system. They've had a few issues that they've had to deal with, but they've been able to respond and come up with solutions."

Nick interrupts, "That's all nice, but it's not gone through our internal approval process. I'm not comfortable signing off on it until the engineering management team has had a chance to review it."

Doreen jumps in. "Nick, no one is trying to cut you and your managers out of the loop. But if we have a solution that appears to work, we can't turn off power to our customers while we go through our approval process. I suggest that we go with what the teams are recommending, and you and your managers can review the work while we're keeping the lights on for customers. If you can pull everyone together tonight, do it, but let's keep moving forward with what the teams are doing."

There is a critical moment for a traditional organization in transition to becoming an agile organization at which it must decide whether to trust the people who are closest to the work to do their jobs. This scenario illustrates that moment in stark contrast: The team members in the NOC and product teams have been working together to solve the problem, and they are closest to the facts, so they are the ones who are best equipped to make a decision. But it is hard for managers in an organization accustomed to top-down control to admit that they are not necessary in this decision-making cycle.

It might be different if the managers were there, working with the teams on the problem. In that case, they might raise questions and spur discussions that could result in better solutions. So long as they are disconnected from the work, however, they don't add anything to the decision-making process.

In this example, the key attribute of the NOC and product teams is that they deeply care about finding solutions to help customers. The managers, with the exception of Doreen and Nagesh, seem to be simply concerned about not looking bad. This is a key indicator that it's time to leave traditional top-down management behind: When agile teams care about customer success, and are measured and rewarded for it, they have the right incentives to make decisions about their work.

Once teams have the skills, knowledge, and motivation to be accountable for customer success, agile leaders can shift their attention to supporting and growing the capabilities of those teams. No team will be perfect in its decisions, just as no person, regardless of their status or role, is perfect in their decisions. Agile teams, however, are much better suited to inspecting and adapting their results and ways of working based on feedback. In addition, the collected brain capacity of such a team is most certainly much higher than any single person has available. Agile leaders need to shift their attention to nurturing their team's ability to inspect and adapt, and thereby grow.

As this scenario suggests, the transition between traditional top-down leadership and empowered teams using bottom-up intelligence is often externally triggered: In every organization that is developing its agile capabilities, there will come a moment when some external crisis reveals that the teams are ready to step up and take on new responsibilities. Much as organizations might like for this transition to occur gradually, external events will intercede. The key challenge for agile leaders is to prepare themselves and their teams for this moment, when it will be time for the leader to let go of managing and to allow the teams to manage themselves. By doing this, the leader has more time available to identify and help solve team-overarching problems.

REFLECTIONS ON THE JOURNEY

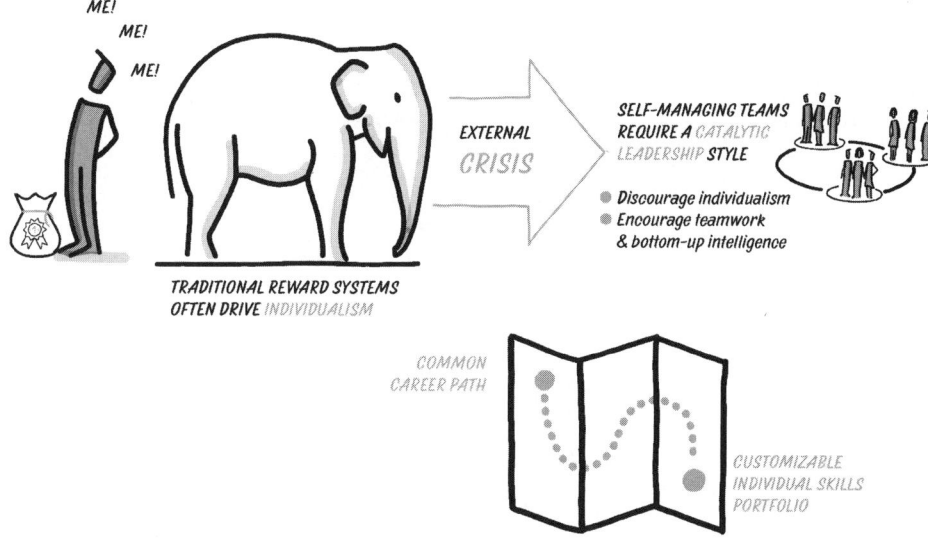

Traditional organizations reward individual performance. They cultivate a narrative that describes how individual heroes overcame great odds to achieve great things. The reality is quite different, though: Not only in our modern world, but throughout all of human history, it has proved virtually impossible for a person to achieve anything on their own without collaborating with others.

Agile leaders who find themselves in these "hero cultures" must find a way to change the narrative to recognize the simple fact that it is teams, not heroes, that get things done. Organizations that cling to their hero narratives find this truth hard to embrace, and the change usually is hardest for leaders who lack a "catalytic" leadership style and see themselves as the essential heroes in their organization's success narrative.

Focusing on team success does not mean that individual contributions are unimportant, but it does reframe that contribution in terms of how it helps the team achieve its goals and reach higher levels of performance. In some ways, teams help to liberate individuals from "one size fits all" career paths and help them to develop their own personal skills in ways that best benefit their teams.

LEADERS, EVERYWHERE

One of the hallmarks of an agile organization is a minimum of hierarchy, coupled with autonomy for teams to do whatever it takes to deliver value for customers. Chapter 5 highlighted how this creates tension in the traditional organization's management hierarchy, as managers feel threatened by having their authority undermined. The case study also illustrated the benefits of helping agile teams to self-organize, which allowed the case study team to apply what they had learned to help quickly solve challenging problems that the traditional management hierarchy hadn't anticipated and to which it couldn't respond.

For organizations to achieve enterprise agility, they have to let go of the idea that leadership is a quality that is possessed by a very small group of people, and embrace the idea that nearly everyone is born with leadership capabilities. Circumstances in combination with the right leadership style will determine if these capabilities will emerge. The role of the agile leader, in this new organization, is to help grow the ability of people in the organization to exercise leadership.

NURTURING AND GROWING AN AGILE ORGANIZATION

The December blackout received a lot of negative attention in the press. There was widespread criticism of the government for lax regulatory oversight, and there were calls for more stringent regulations on energy companies. Traditional energy companies were also singled out as being too greedy to invest in maintaining and updating their infrastructure, and too incompetent to anticipate the causes of the outage. Although Reliable Energy bore some of this unwanted attention along with other traditional energy companies, there was also a recognition in the press that it had done some different things that enabled the company to respond to the outage in innovative ways.

Doreen's own agile journey took a major turn in the aftermath of the blackout. She had seen how the traditional organization had become stuck in its own processes and bureaucracy, while the nascent agile teams had responded with creativity and enthusiasm. Their response bolstered her resolve to break down the old organization and build a truly agile organization. She began to look for new ways and opportunities to move the whole organization toward the agile future that she now knew was inevitable.

Because of the blackout, all competitors, including Reliable Energy, failed to meet the long-planned end-of-year tender deadlines for the multi-country Smart Grid initiative. But for Reliable Energy, there was an upside: The agile teams' experience in responding to the blackout gave them valuable insights into how to avoid these kinds of events in the future. That knowledge informed a major revision to the company's tender proposal as the teams pushed ahead to deliver their tender response, though late, before any of the other competitors.

By mid-January, with the blackout and tender response behind them, Doreen and Nagesh are discussing how to grow agility throughout the organization. Nagesh is drawing on a whiteboard.

"The biggest mistake I've seen organizations make is that once they start seeing success from their agile teams, they become frustrated with how long it takes to help a team reach a high level of performance. They start to look for shortcuts, and they start doing things differently than they did with the agile teams that are just starting to show success."

Doreen nods. "I understand the pressure. After our success with the blackout and the tender offer, the board is pressuring me to ramp up our agility very quickly."

Nagesh starts to draw. "There is a way to systematically launch and grow agile teams. It's not that hard, but it requires patience. If you remember, we started the GSS team by letting them choose their own members. We shouldn't change that as we move ahead; it's important to help teams do that as the first step toward self-management. We can help them with coaching to make the process easier, but we can't hurry it up by assigning people to teams."

Doreen adds, "We should include all the stakeholders in that team-forming process. Not just keeping them in the loop, but making them active participants. We stumbled a bit at first because we didn't do that." (See Figure 6.1.)

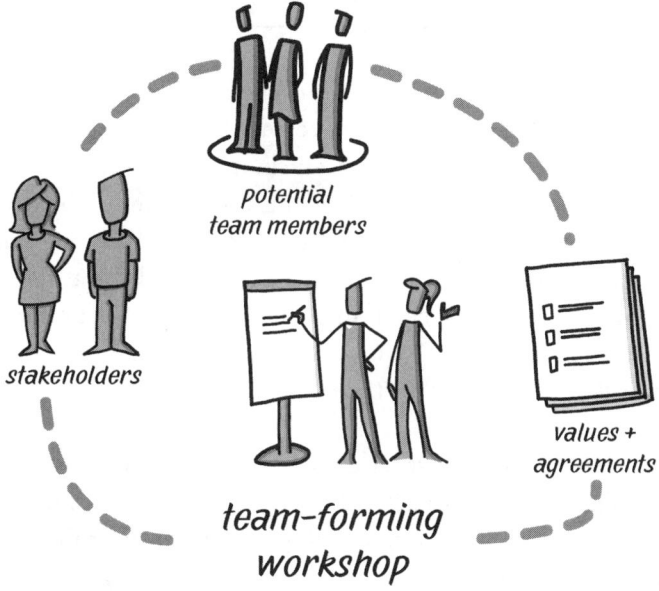

Figure 6.1 Workshops can be used to help teams to form and self-organize.

Nagesh continues, "Based on what we now know, I think we can develop a workshop that helps teams to form, to build strong working relationships with their stakeholders, and to help the teams learn how to better manage themselves."

Doreen sees where Nagesh was going with this. "Yes, it did take a while for our teams to learn how to self-manage, and for their stakeholders to learn how to work with them. I can see how such a workshop could help. I can also see how it would help to build the commitment of stakeholders to help their teams to remove impediments."

> Nagesh responds, "Exactly. If we can get other people in the organization to feel ownership for the success of the teams, we will go a long way toward instilling agility in the broader organization. You and I can't be the sole proponents of this change; we need to enlist the help of other leaders in the organization."
>
> Doreen agrees, "Having this team formation workshop will make it much easier for us to start up new teams and new initiatives. We should think about how we might ask people from the existing agile teams to help as facilitators or ask one of the experienced facilitators from Energy Bridge to guide them. Their experience will give them a lot of insight into how to help a new team that is just forming, and it will give them the credibility that they need to be effective facilitators."

We gave a glimpse of the team formation process in Chapter 2, focusing on team member self-selection and team self-management. A more complete picture of team formation needs to include stakeholders, because without their support and engagement, agile teams are unable to function effectively when they have to work with other parts of the organization. Stakeholders need to buy into not only team self-management, but also the agile development approach that delivers small increments of working product at frequent intervals to real customers. If they don't, the agile team will wither from lack of support and start merely "faking" agility.

These stakeholders must have the respect of the rest of the organization as well. They will need to ask others in the organization for help on behalf of the team, and if they cannot "call in favors" to get things done, the agile team will also languish. In addition, agile teams will engage with people throughout the organization who can help to provide information, but they need well-placed, politically influential stakeholders to help clear obstacles and to provide guidance. When agile teams fail, it is often because they lack senior leadership's support for what they are trying to accomplish.

Agile teams often fail due to a lack of senior leadership's support.

As mentioned in Chapter 2, team members should not be assigned to teams; they need to choose to be part of a team. That goes for stakeholders, too. If people really don't buy into the idea of letting teams self-manage, or if they don't want to work with the other team members, they won't fully engage. Worse, they may even undermine the team's work, albeit possibly unintentionally.

During the team-building workshop, it should be acceptable to have a potential team member or stakeholder decide that they don't want to be a part of the team or the initiative. Establishing this permission can be challenging in organizational cultures that reward "positive attitude." A skilled facilitator with experience in team self-selection may have to help surface the concerns if they perceive that someone is not fully engaged, and they must create space for team members and stakeholders to disengage if they feel that's what is best for them.

Scaling Team Formation

Leaders in organizations who have seen the power of an effective, high-performing, self-managing team can sometimes inadvertently create a new problem. Once sold on the need for self-management, they may be impatient with the time and investment they have seen it takes to grow a high-performing team. In short, they may be looking for a shortcut that will trim the time and effort to a fraction of what the original team took, so that they can rapidly change hundreds of teams in their organization. To use an analogy from science fiction, they want a "warp drive"— something that will allow them to suspend the laws of physics and arrive instantaneously at a distant goal.

Let's be blunt: There is no shortcut that eliminates all the time and effort of helping a team to grow its ability to self-manage. If there were, the organization would have used it in the first place.

To go further, the surest way to destroy an organization's ability to become agile is to try to take a shortcut and start up lots of agile teams all at once. Organizations that try this approach spread themselves too thin and raise expectations to unachievable levels. The resulting crash when the organization realizes that its expectations are wildly unrealistic usually creates antagonism toward the agile approach from which it cannot recover.

Instead of looking for a magical shortcut, just get started. Help grow one successful team. And then another. And then a few more. Each experience will make the next one easier, and instead of recovering from a hangover of magical thinking, the organization will actually have a solid foundation of experience on which it can build.

Support Agile Teams with the Right Skills, at the Right Time

As they formed more agile teams, Doreen discovered another challenge they had to overcome. "No matter how cross-functional the agile team is, the team members still need outside help sometimes. All the teams are working hard to improve their cross-functional skills, but there is always something that comes up that causes them to need someone with skills or authority that they don't have to make decisions. The way we work today, that means that they have to wait for someone to free up time to help them, and those people are usually very busy helping other teams."

Nagesh agrees. "It's really killing the morale of the teams. They can see how they really can't be successful if they have to wait on the rest of the organization all the time."

Doreen starts drawing three columns on the whiteboard. "Here is how I view what we've done so far." (See Figure 6.2.) "This first column represents the first few agile teams we formed after we acquired Energy Bridge. The teams were fairly independent and cross-functional, but they couldn't deliver an entire 'done' product[1] on their own; they needed the help of the operations and infrastructure teams, which were largely stuck in traditional silos."

She continues, drawing a second column. "Then, during the blackout crisis, the teams started involving some of the other disciplines that were needed to complete a product end-to-end. In responding to the blackout, the boundaries between teams faded, and even after the blackout was over, the people on each of the teams tended to work with each other more fluidly, without needing to go through official channels, even though they were officially part of separate teams. But it took an emergency to form these bonds, and we can already see them fading over time."

Now drawing a third column, Doreen continues. "We need to figure out a way to break down these barriers and let teams work more independently, owning the entire value stream from idea to customer experience. We've started to see a new model evolving, where 'experts' float between teams, wherever they are needed, but only as long as they are needed. A few people are working this way, even though they still report into their old teams. We need to find a way to support and encourage this. Our current system punishes this sort of behavior."

---

1. See this blog to find out what "done" means: www.scrum.org/resources/blog/done-understanding-definition-done.

Nagesh agrees. "Yes, we also saw this at Energy Bridge, early on. What we found, and what I've heard from colleagues at other organizations doing similar things, is that for teams to really become self-managing and accountable for customer outcomes, they have to own the entire value chain. Over time, that means some of the teams that we have today, which exist to provide a place for specialized skills to live, will have to be disbanded. Some of those skills, such as hiring or supporting products, will have to be taken on by agile teams because they need to have those core skills to be successful. Other skills that are more specialized and used less frequently, such as legal knowledge or information security, might remain separate, but they always need to be available to agile teams when they need them. This means we might need to increase our staffing in those areas so that agile teams don't have to wait."

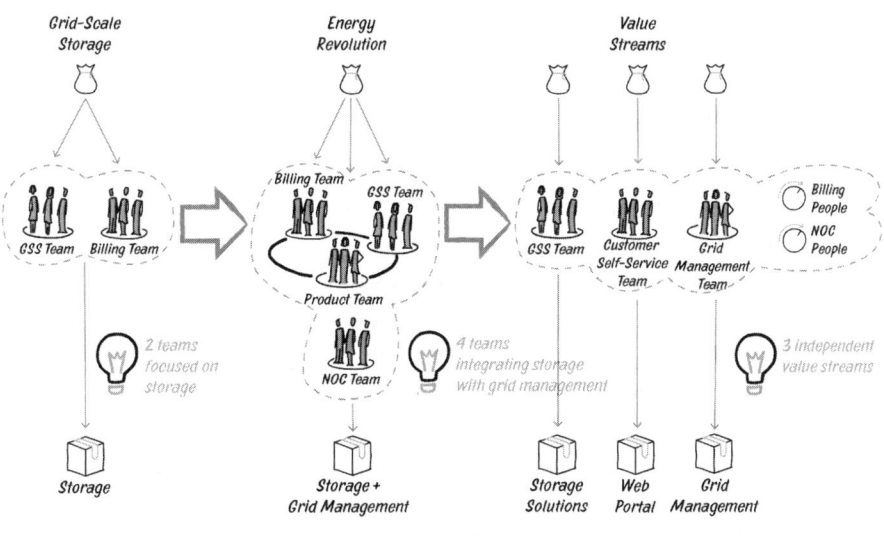

Figure 6.2 Team organizational structures must evolve for agile teams to evolve and grow.

The third column of Figure 6.2 shows an important way that organizations break down their silos. Instead of having separate NOC and Billing teams, with accompanying coordination challenges, the GSS, Customer Self-Service, and Grid Management teams simply need to have people with Billing and NOC expertise available when they need them. These people temporarily join the teams to provide expertise and skills that the teams lack. They leave the teams when they are no longer needed, either because the need has passed or because they helped the teams to grow their own expertise.

The key to making this work is the phrase "available when they need them." When agile teams have to file a request and wait for someone to become available to help them, they experience delays that render them ineffective. Agile leaders need to work with teams to anticipate their demands for scarce skills, and then find ways to make the right people available at the right time.

ORGANIZATIONAL SILOS IMPEDE AGILITY AND PRODUCTIVITY

Traditional organizations build teams around sets of related skills. Such teams are sometimes referred to as "silos" because they tend to stand alone, only loosely connected to other silos. These silos exist because the organization believes that having specialized skills is valuable, and that managing a particular set of specialized skills requires a unique focus, one that is different from managing a different set of skills. Once the organization goes down this path, it will promote employees within these areas of skill specialization.

This siloed organization produces several unhappy results:

- It discourages employees from developing broadly cross-functional skills.
- It makes forming and growing cross-functional teams almost impossible because a cross-functional team formed of specialists would be too large to be effective.
- It results in teams composed of part-time members, which slows down work. Since a cross-functional team of specialists leaves most team

members idle at any one time, organizations that try to form teams with specialist members almost always have people belong to multiple teams. The more teams a person is on, the more scheduling conflicts they will experience, resulting in large amounts of idle time spent waiting to work with other team members.

- It also results in a promotional reward system that favors narrow, specialized skills over cross-functional, generalist skills.

No wonder traditional organizations take a very long time to get a very small amount of work done! And no wonder that cross-functional teams are so difficult to sustain over time; the system is rigged against them.

CROSS-FUNCTIONAL TEAMS IMPROVE PRODUCTIVITY, BUT STILL NEED SUPPORT

Agile teams solve these problems by forming cross-functional teams and encouraging their team members to further broaden and deepen their skills. This reduces wait time and improves the team's ability to get work done quickly.

Such cross-functionality has limits because a team must remain fairly small, typically having no more than nine members, to remain effective, and there are only so many things at which a person can be truly skilled. In addition, there will always be deep skills that may require years of training to master, and that will not make sense for a team member to acquire. Examples include skills in the law, in medicine, in engineering, and in other technical areas.

The solution to this problem is illustrated by the third column in Figure 6.2: The people with scarce but important skills must, in a sense, support the agile teams, waiting for opportunities to help the teams with work they need to do. This is comparable to a firefighter who eagerly waits for the moment to resolve a possible crisis, but also helps people to avoid the crisis in the first place by giving fire-prevention advice. This model differs from the traditional model in an important way: In the agile model, specialists wait on agile teams to serve them when they need help, while in the traditional model, agile teams wait on specialists to become available. While specialists are often highly paid, having them be idle sometimes is much more cost-effective than having entire teams wait.

The key to making the agile-specialist model work is that enough specialists need to be available so that agile teams don't have to wait. This results in an uncomfortable situation for both the specialists and the organization's management: They have to become comfortable with having highly paid people who are waiting for work to come to them. Choosing the right number of specialists means balancing specialist waiting time against agile team waiting time to reach an optimal balance.

Specialist "Downtime" Can Be Used to Improve Team Effectiveness

Specialists with some kinds of scarce skills can use the time they would otherwise spend waiting by being helpful—that is, by building solutions that can help the teams support themselves:

- Software security specialists can build automated tests that can be added to continuous integration automation to catch common flaws early in the delivery process. The same can be done for many other concerns, such as performance, reliability, scalability, and other aspects of product quality.[2]
- Legal professionals can organize or create educational materials on topics that can help educate agile team members on basic concepts related to protecting intellectual property, including what they need to do, at a minimum, and when they need to seek professional advice.

---

2. It is beyond the scope of this book to discuss continuous software integration and delivery practices. For an excellent introduction to these concepts and practices, see https://continuousdelivery.com/.

- Operations professionals can create tools to support automated deployment and can provide frameworks for instrumenting applications for supportability.
- Human resources professionals can provide educational materials and guidance to help teams become better at recruitment and team building.

In short, people with specialized skills should be working toward helping agile teams to become more self-sufficient, and to know when to ask for help. Organizations transitioning to an agile working model may want to outsource some of these specialized functions, using outside consultants and coaches to provide flexibility in staffing where proprietary knowledge is not required. The key to making this approach successful is that while asset-building is important, it should always be undertaken in service of helping teams to become more self-sufficient.

Specialists Need to Stay Connected with the Teams They Support

Teams may not always know when they need help. To overcome the "we don't know what we don't know" problem, specialists need to stay closely connected with the teams they support. Having specialists attend team daily meetings when they are not busy helping a particular team is one way to do this without a lot of overhead. They often find ways to engage immediately, as issues arise. Participating in agile planning events is another way the specialists can engage with agile team members to understand when and how they can best help.

Another way to have specialists support the teams is through pull-requests for coaching, using an IT infrastructure to support these requests. Companies like Buurtzorg Nederland have created an environment where self-governing teams can thrive using such a support combination. Buurtzorg Nederland's 13,500 employees do not work within a typical top-down management structure. Instead, by implementing a very flat management structure, this company has created a clear governance system in which coaches support the teams in their needs, but all management decisions are made by the self-managing teams.

Despite the lack of traditional top-down control mechanisms, scope and duties have remained manageable in Buurtzorg Nederland thanks to small team sizes, an IT system that keeps operational burdens to a minimum, and on-demand guidance from regional coaches. Using the company's cloud-based infrastructure, teams can continuously communicate with the specialists. All information (e.g., client files, planning, learning environment, team status) is made transparent in this infrastructure.

With this different leadership approach and supporting infrastructure, Buurtzorg Nederland has been very successful. Since the company was founded in 2006, it has scaled from 1 to 900 independent teams (as of 2018), caring for more than 70,000 patients per year and owning 20% of its market.[3]

SPECIALISTS WORK PRIMARILY AS TEACHERS, COACHES, AND MENTORS, NOT "DOERS"

While it's easiest for a specialist to simply jump in and "do the work," that doesn't help the agile team to improve its self-sufficiency. It's better if the specialist works with team members to improve their skills so that they can do the work in the future. Practices such as pairing up are a great way to accomplish this goal. Teaching and coaching are the most important skills for specialists who support teams. If the specialist has been accustomed to being an individual contributor in the past, they may need help to improve their teaching and coaching skills. Working with the agile team also offers specialists a growth opportunity to improve their own leadership skills, since leadership typically involves teaching, coaching, and mentoring in both direct and indirect ways.

LEADERSHIP JOURNEYS: DEVELOPING LEADERS EVERYWHERE

One of the most important roles of leaders and specialists in the organization is to make sure that teams have enough opportunities to learn the skills they need to be successful.

---

3. For more information about Buurtzorg Nederland's model, see www.buurtzorg.com/about-us/buurtzorgmodel/.

Teams that operate in a complex domain will find themselves in continuous need of learning new skills, and leaders need to provide an infrastructure that facilitates this learning. In this way, teams can grow and leaders are created everywhere in the organization.

Leadership is an activity, not a role, and the role of leaders is to help other leaders to grow.

Traditional organizations often outsource their training and education activities, but in a knowledge economy, success strongly depends on each employee's ability to gain new knowledge and skills. Agile leaders should ask themselves how they can incorporate skills in managing intellectual capital into their teams. In a world where more and more skilled people are changing jobs, employers who understand how to manage their intellectual capital effectively have a competitive advantage.[4] The catalytic leadership style (described in Chapter 5 and illustrated in Figure 5.1) is more likely to attract leaders who can contribute to a culture of knowledge sharing and creativity.

In organizations that rely on self-organizing teams, professionals often need to embark on a lifelong learning journey in which they continuously learn new skills.[5] An analogy that is often used is a tree, where the trunk represents common knowledge that a person needs on this journey, while the branches and leaves represent specialties and unique skills that keep changing over the course of the individual's career.

Figure 6.3 highlights some of the skills that are typically required in an agile environment. As it suggests, different roles will require different skills. Not only do organizations need to provide opportunities for their people to get trained in these skills, but leaders also need to provide learning opportunities for employees to practice, master, and become experts in these skills.

---

4. https://hrexecutive.com/one-in-4-workers-plans-to-quit-post-pandemic/.
5. https://link.springer.com/chapter/10.1007/978-3-319-28868-0_10/.

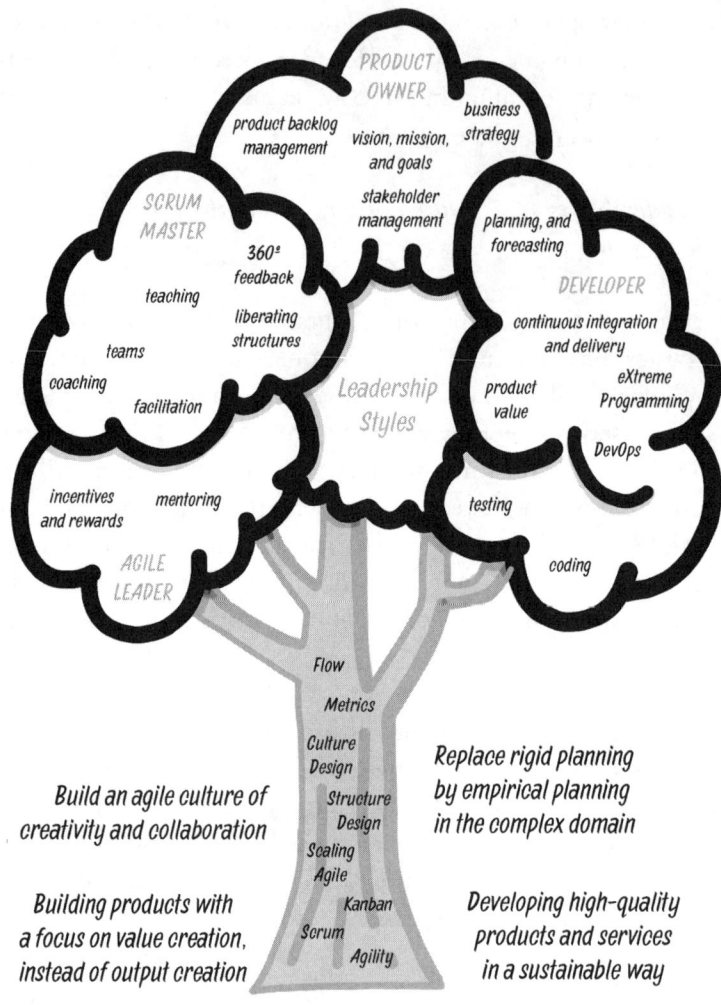

Figure 6.3 Examples of skills required in an agile environment.

Figure 6.4 gives an overview of the different learning methods that can be used to support people and teams on their continuous learning journey.

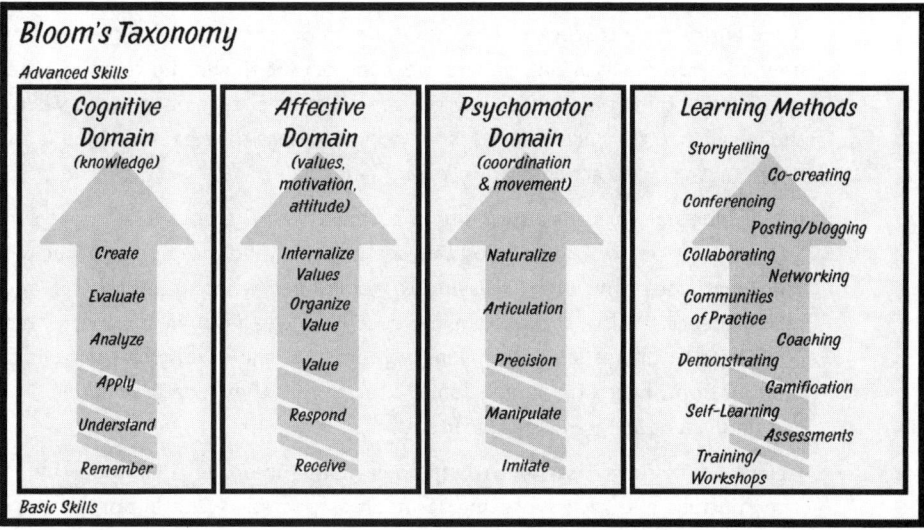

Figure 6.4 Bloom's taxonomy describes a set of models, named after Benjamin Bloom, who chaired the committee of educators that devised the taxonomy.

Figure 6.4 shows an overview of models used by educators to design learning methods. While most organizations apply the basic learning methods, they focus less on the learning methods that lead to a higher level of skills. Organizations and leaders who stimulate their employees to apply the higher-level learning methods can expect a boost in their teams' ability to self-organize and learn new skills faster.

The Myth of Multitasking

Some people will say, at this point, that agile teams are not adversely affected by having to wait on a specialist or "expert," that they can always work on other things while they are waiting. These same people may also say that having employees be members of many teams helps to solve this problem because if one team a person is assigned to is "stuck waiting," that person can simply do work for some other team on which they work.

Both of these beliefs lead to waste.

If the entire team is stuck waiting, focusing on other work usually means that team members are not working on the most important thing. The team may be working on something that, once they get specialist help, turns out to be valueless. At the very least, they are delayed in working on what they have decided is the most important thing to accomplish to meet their goals.

If individuals are assigned to multiple teams, there is a cost to context switching: Every time a person starts one task, sets it aside, and picks up another task, that individual loses time due to having to remember where they left off once they pick it up again. Also, think about the cost of having a double amount of meetings, conflicting priorities, tools, working agreements, and so on. The same is true for interruptions: Every time a person is interrupted, they lose productivity owing to the time spent in regaining their focus.[6]

Agile leaders should strive to help their teams improve their focus by reducing interruptions and task switching as much as possible. One important way to do this is to improve the cross-functionality of agile teams, and to fill skills gaps with outside help so that the team doesn't need to queue up for that help.

REWARD BUILDING TEAMS AND LEADERSHIP, NOT SILOS

To support the shift of specialists from "doers" to coaches, teachers, and mentors, Doreen realizes that she also needs the managers of these specialists to change their focus. To that end, she announces changes to the way that executives are evaluated at an executive staff meeting.

In the past, executives and managers were evaluated on their delivery of key initiatives in their departments. Since agile teams are cross-functional, departmental initiatives no longer make sense. Instead, Doreen plans to evaluate executives and managers based on how they help to grow the capabilities of agile teams.

The result is predictable but, to Doreen, disappointing. Nick is one of the most vocal opponents and expresses what a lot of the other executives are thinking.

---

6. For more information about the cost of interruptions, see www.washingtonpost.com/news/inspired-life/ wp/2015/06/01/interruptions-at-work-can-cost-you-up-to-6-hours-a-day-heres-how-to-avoid-them/.

"We've already lost a lot of the people who used to work for us when they joined agile teams. Now you want to hold us accountable for the performance of teams that don't even report to us? To me, all this just looks like bad management, with the inmates running the asylum."

Doreen pauses for a moment to make sure that Nick is done venting, and to let anyone else jump in. They are silent, waiting to see how she responds.

"Nick, I'm sure you didn't mean to imply that our organization is some kind of mental institution," Doreen says, smiling, to try to diffuse some of the frustration.

She continues, "We've seen our teams do some great things since we started shifting to cross-functional, self-managing teams. I've had some of our most outspoken critics in the past come up to me in the hallways and say that the past 6 months have been the most professionally rewarding time in their careers. We're seeing the kind of real commitment and engagement from our teams that we've never really seen before. I don't want to throw that away so we can go back to our old way of working."

She pauses, letting that sink in, and looks for reactions. A number of executives seem to be agreeing. Even Nick seems to grudgingly agree. She continues, "I think you're selling yourselves short. Each of you has tremendous experience and perspectives to share with these teams. You're all incredibly successful, and we need more people like you. Helping other people to grow, to do the amazing things that you can do, is the greatest contribution you can make to this company. We're at a critical point in our history, and the only way we're going to survive and thrive is to channel all the energy, creativity, and passion of *all* of our team members toward reaching our goals."

"What I'm asking you to do is to help develop our teams. If their decision-making skills need work, help them to develop them. If they need help clearing obstacles, help them to clear them, then help them to do it for themselves the next time. We have so much that needs to be done; we all need to work together. That means us, too."

Doreen pauses there to wait for the reaction. She is prepared for Nick to continue arguing for a return to the old ways, but he surprises her. He takes a moment, and his expression softens. "Okay. I'm sorry to have reacted the way that I did. These changes just keep coming so fast that it's hard not to feel overwhelmed. How can I help? How can *we* help each other?"

It can be hard for some managers to let go of the perceived status that comes with directing other people. Senior leaders can subtly shift the organization's culture by helping the *whole* organization see that a leader's influence extends far beyond their direct management chain and formal authority. Leading *is* different from managing, especially in the potential positive impact that leaders can create.

In this example, Doreen makes a conscious decision to change the way that managers are rewarded to explicitly recognize the value that leaders can create when they help other people to learn and grow. Traditional management always has an aspect of professional growth, but it tends to emphasize the individual contributions of managers, not the amplified but indirect contribution they make by helping others to become more effective.

During this transition, some managers will feel that their authority, and therefore their status, is being undermined. They may feel undervalued. Some may leave. But those who embrace their new responsibilities as teacher, coach, and mentor will find that their ability to influence the results the organization is able to achieve has been multiplied by the force of all the people whom they help.

Many of us live and work in cultures in which the individual is preeminent, yet the truth is that no one—not even the most capable of individuals—can get much done without the help of others. Our ability to influence the world for good relies on our ability to form teams with others to get things done. Agile leaders create the space for agile teams to form, learn, and grow, so that they, in turn, can exhibit leadership. Agile teams need support, but perhaps even more importantly, they need good examples of how real servant leadership works.

Agile teams need good examples of how real servant leadership works.

PROMOTIONAL REWARDS LOCK IN ORGANIZATIONAL STRUCTURES

Organizations throughout history have used promotion as one way to reward people for exceptional performance. Promotions usually confer increased status as well as increases in monetary compensation. Promotions also tend to lock an organization into a particular hierarchical structure that is hard to change when the nature of the work changes.

In the case study, Nick is head of the engineering organization, which in the past has meant that all developers report to Nick's organization. As Reliable Energy has adopted cross-functional teams, many people may have development skills who are not necessarily developers. As people acquire diverse skills, the old organizational structure no longer serves the needs of the organization. This creates conflict within the ranks of all the former managers in the engineering organization.

A more flexible model is to focus teams on delivering a set of outcomes to a group of customers who have common needs. As the customers' needs change, so, too, may the teams. But the organization in which these teams work is fairly flat; it doesn't need a lot of layers of management. As teams develop their ability to self-manage, there are fewer opportunities for promotional rewards. This can cause a bit of a crisis in terms of the whole notion of careers and organizational progression.

Without promotional opportunities, organizations have to find other ways to reward and motivate their employees, principally by giving people a greater sense of purpose by defining meaningful goals, increasing the autonomy of people in how they reach those goals, and recognizing mastery and professionalism. Employees need to feel that they are being paid fairly for their contributions, but beyond that most professionals engaged in knowledge work seek intrinsic rewards. For leaders, recognition based on demonstrated achievements in helping teams to improve their performance and effectiveness provides a better way to recognize their contributions.

What About Bonuses?

In domains in which self-managed teams continuously solve complex problems, bonuses are not an effective way of rewarding people. The nature of complex work is such that organizations are not able to predict the future, so it is impossible to set bonus targets. In fact, for teams that do complex work, bonuses are actually counterproductive.

As a leader, it's important to make sure that employees are focused on what is best for the company at any time, rather than working toward some bonus target that was created a year ago, based on false assumptions. It is better to hire the best people and pay them an above-average salary, so they can shift their focus from achieving a bonus based on arbitrary criteria to doing the work at hand.

If you want to reward people for their contributions, team-based rewards that share some of the profit that the team has helped to generate make more sense. Or just pay salaries above the market rate for people with their skills, as Netflix has, and abandon the whole bonus charade in the first place.[7]

PERFORMANCE REVIEWS DON'T GO AWAY, BUT THEY DO CHANGE DRAMATICALLY

In an agile organization, evaluating individual performance doesn't go away, but rather is based on the perceptions of an employee's fellow team members rather than the opinion of a manager. In fact, the traditional annual performance review process is so widely and justly criticized that no one should be unhappy to see it retired.[8]

Instead of relying on infrequent feedback from people who really don't work with a person, agile organizations are shifting toward frequent (i.e., quarterly or more frequently) feedback from an employee's fellow team members and

---

7. In their book *No Rules Rules*, Reed Hastings (Netflix's CEO) and Erin Meyer explain how and why Netflix abandoned a number of traditional mechanisms like the bonus system in an effort to stay ahead of their competition and keep innovating.

8. For more on the widespread unhappiness with traditional performance reviews, see www.gallup.com/workplace/249332/harm-good-truth-performance-reviews.aspx.

other colleagues. One popular approach is the 360-degree feedback session.[9] The important aspects of these sessions are that they are frequent, so that they provide feedback close to a specific event, and they include at least several different perspectives, to provide a balanced view of performance.

The main goal of 360-degree feedback is to use it as input for personal and team improvement. Psychological safety is a precondition for team members to give honest and constructive feedback. Agile leaders set the preconditions to accomplish this goal.

The following examples demonstrate how the authors have assisted teams with their 360-degree reviews. In both examples, the feedback is collected by a leader in a team whose members have high-trust relationships with each other. Based on this relationship, the team leader facilitates the process and gives feedback, but also receives feedback from fellow team members. Our role is to help these team leaders to facilitate these sessions, learn from each other, and improve their facilitation skills.

COLLECTING FEEDBACK WITH A QUESTIONNAIRE THROUGH AN APP

To make sure feedback is used for personal improvement in a safe space, it needs to be uncoupled from incentives. Using an app that is accessible to a neutral/nonhierarchical assessor (such as the team leader) and team members only to collect feedback is one way to obtain such feedback in a neutral and anonymous way. Our experiments with this have followed a pattern:

- Each feedback round contains self-reflection and gives input to all team members. The difference between self-reflection and team feedback creates interesting insights for personal growth.

---

9. For more information on this technique, see https://evolutionaryleadership.nl/leadership/360-feedback/.

- In teams with established psychological safety, feedback is collected and shared as a group. In other teams, we start more safely with individual sessions and anonymous input.
- The feedback system checks a number of (customizable) criteria, such as being a good team player, personal values, and team diversity.

The result of a fictitious feedback session for an individual is shown in Figure 6.5, with the average for the teams feedback shown as a bar, and the individual's self-assessment superimposed as a line. Differences between the team's average and the individual's self-assessment provide the foundation for discussion with the individual about the differences.

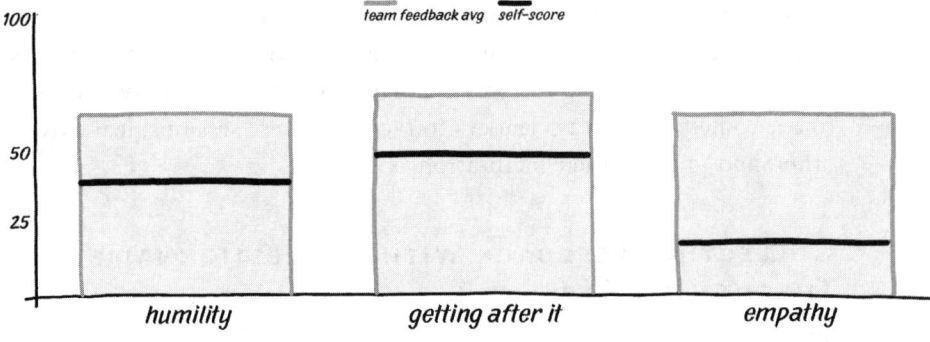

Figure 6.5 An illustration of a 360-degree feedback session. A combination of introspection and peer feedback can expose great opportunities for professional growth.

Collecting Feedback by Playing a "Game"

Another way to facilitate 360-degree feedback in a team is to gamify the feedback process. We developed a card game[10] that helps teams to facilitate the feedback process, as illustrated in Figure 6.6:

---

10. For more information on this game, see https://evolutionaryleadership.nl/leadership/core-qualities/.

- Teams that are still developing psychological safety give each other feedback based on qualities.
- Teams with an established psychological safety can add distortion/challenges cards to the mix.

The insights from this card game have helped many teams and team members to discover their challenges, discover conflicts, and resolve them. The example in Figure 6.6 illustrates the result of such a feedback session.

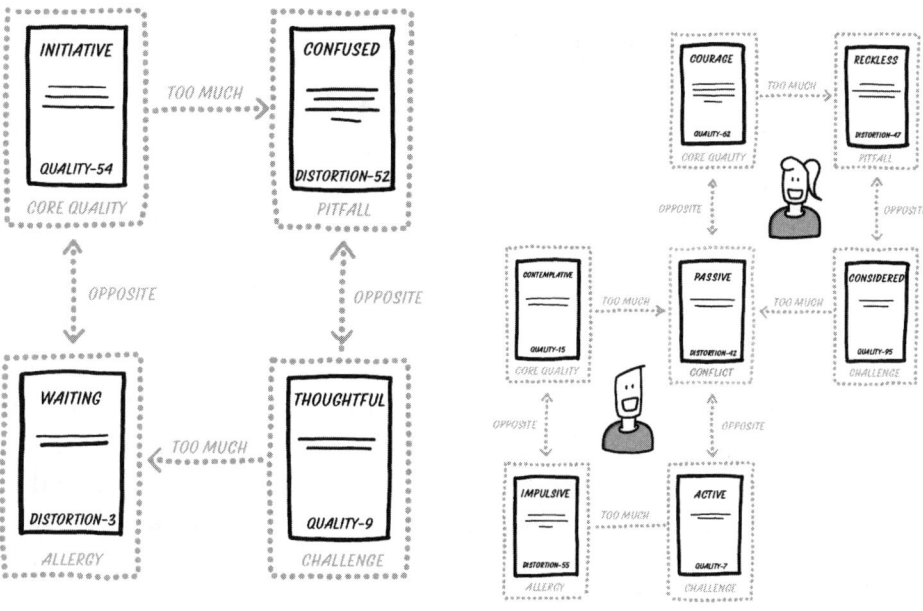

Figure 6.6 An example of a 360-feedback session, using our card game with Core Qualities.

REFLECTIONS ON THE JOURNEY

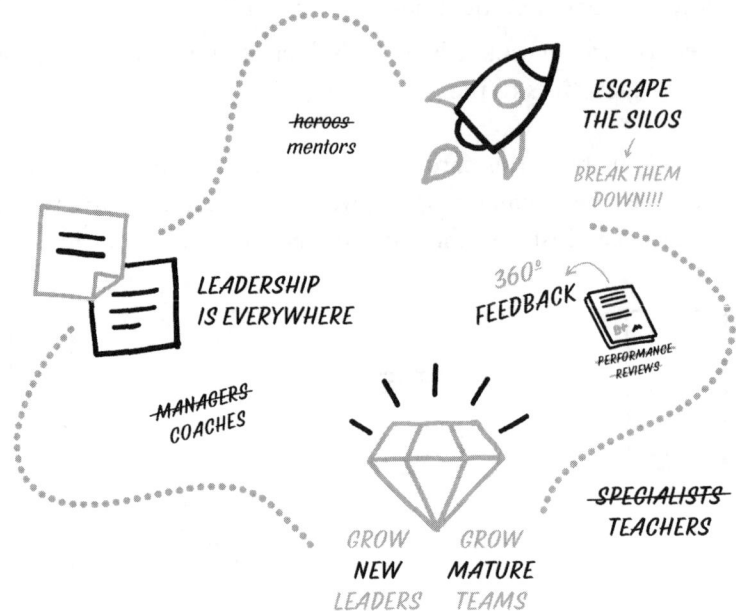

Helping teams to learn and grow requires leaders to work in different ways and requires others who may not think of themselves as leaders to develop their own leadership skills. Traditional managers grow their own agile leadership skills by shifting their focus from managing and overseeing work to coaching teams and supporting them as they learn new ways to work.

Team members who have, in the past, focused on developing specialized technical skills also grow their leadership skills by helping their fellow team members learn and apply those skills in situations where the team will benefit from having more people with those skills. This is the opposite of what they would do if they were in a "siloed" organization that seeks to differentiate itself by the scarce skills that it controls.

Traditional managers also grow their agile leadership skills by letting go of individual performance reviews and helping teams to assess the contributions of their own members using 360-degree feedback techniques. Many, if not most, managers will find this liberating, since it frees the manager from having to assess an individual's performance when they have little opportunity to directly observe that individual in the performance of their job.

ALIGNING THE
ORGANIZATION

As organizations grow their agility, team by team, product by product, they come to a point where they must either fully commit to continuing their agile journey or they will fall back to the old ways of working. Organizations can continue for a long time with two different operating models, one agile and one traditional, coexisting side-by-side. But they cannot maintain these two models forever; they are incompatible and diametrically opposed. They create and demand opposing cultures. Eventually, one culture or the other will win out.

> The "dual operating system" approach[1] is a false dichotomy; there is no part of the organization that will not benefit from self-managing teams. The challenge is in helping teams that are just getting started with self-management to learn and grow.

In our consulting work, we have met with many executives who told us that their organizations had tried to become agile, but "it didn't work for them." When we visited these organizations, we witnessed very little evidence that

---

1. https://hbr.org/2012/11/accelerate.

they had even attempted to adopt an agile approach; they seemed as trapped by tradition as organizations that had never even attempted agility.

What these executives really meant when they said "agile didn't work for them" is that their organizations were unwilling to confront the hard realities of agile change: There are winners and losers in the shift to agility, and failing to acknowledge this makes change harder.

Previous chapters have touched on aspects of this issue, because it comes up at predictable points along an organization's agile journey. This chapter returns to this topic, with greater focus. As an organization proves the value of agility to itself, and as it grows its agile capabilities, there will come a point when it has to choose. This chapter is about making that choice.

For leaders, the essence of this transformation is to eliminate combative and compliant leadership styles, while helping people with competitive leadership style to develop a catalytic leadership style. So long as the leaders in the organization cling to combative, compliant, or competitive leadership styles, the organization will never fully achieve its agile potential.

EVOLVING THE OPERATING MODEL

> Over the next six months, Reliable Energy launches a handful of new self-managing teams in the same way as it did initially, by finding people who want to work in a new way and then helping them to come together as a team. Morale on these teams is high, and the results they produce sometimes surprise even the new team members.
>
> The success of these teams creates a different problem: What was once an agile cell is now gradually becoming mainstream. Some employees in established parts of the organization are unhappy and resentful of the attention and visibility given to the teams in this new part of the organization. Some of these employees don't see a need to change and resent the implication that they have been performing poorly, necessitating a different approach. Other employees, who want to try working in a new way, are frustrated because they feel blocked by management from joining a new team.

Managers in the traditional organization are unhappy as well. More than one senior manager has approached Doreen expressing frustration that some of their best employees have been allowed to join agile teams, leaving the traditional managers supporting existing products and services with the same workload but fewer people to do the work. Behind this, though, these managers are worried that the functions that they manage are gradually being taken over by the agile teams themselves, leaving the managers wondering where their careers are headed.

Doreen is getting worn down. She believes that moving to an agile approach is the right thing to do, and the morale of agile team members and the results they are producing have proved her right, but the constant struggle of the traditional organization against the agile organization is exhausting. She raises this issue with Nagesh one day.

"Does it ever get easier?"

Nagesh responds, "Does *what* ever get easier?"

Doreen elaborates, "Change. Will we ever get to the point where we don't have one part of the organization trying to undermine the other?" She is smiling, weakly, but Nagesh can see how weary she has become.

Nagesh takes a moment. He considers responding with a joke, but he can see that she is serious. "No organization can maintain this *dual operating model* forever. The agile model threatens the very foundation of the traditional organization. Traditional organizations are built on silos of specialization, and this specialization creates *turf battles*. The hierarchy of the organization is there not just to manage the specialists, but to ensure that the hierarchy is respected and protected."

Doreen considers this for a moment. "What do you mean?"

Nagesh replies, "Well, let's take marketing, for example. The marketing department wants to make sure that messaging is consistent and controlled. And to some degree, that's a good thing, because we don't want just anyone in the company coming up with their own messaging. Except, ..." and here Nagesh pauses for effect, "having to go through marketing approval channels every time we need to talk to a customer slows down our ability to innovate."

Doreen nods. "But that's why we are working toward having marketing expertise within each of the teams, so they become better at considering messaging in every customer interaction."

> Nagesh agrees, but adds, "Yes, but the people in the old marketing organization feel left out of this. And, right now, they are. We're taking away their mission and leaving them with nothing to manage. And the managers, especially, are watching their careers dissolve in front of their eyes."
>
> Nagesh continues, "The solution is to accelerate the transition to self-managing teams. For the people with skills that the teams don't need all the time, make them coaches and mentors to teams. Give them goals that help them develop other people, and celebrate their contributions to growing people and teams."

BE DIRECT AND CLEAR ABOUT THE CHANGE

The change described in Chapter 5 takes a long time to work its way through the organization. Eventually, the old organization has to be largely dismantled—but if it's dismantled before agile teams can really take on the work, the organization will fail. There are a lot of moving parts to manage, and the work is delicate (see Figure 7.1).

The essence of the process is conceptually simple:

- The organization helps a team to form that can own some complex product or service that delivers one or more outcomes to some group of customers. If this product or service already exists, the mission for that product or service transfers to the new team.
- The organization supports this team with specialist coaches who provide the team with skills the team lacks, when the team needs the help. Over time, these specialists should help team members to acquire the skills so that they no longer need outside help.
- As work is transferred to agile teams, the traditional organization needs to shrink. What is left, in the end, tends to be executive functions and coaches focused on organization direction and organizational development.

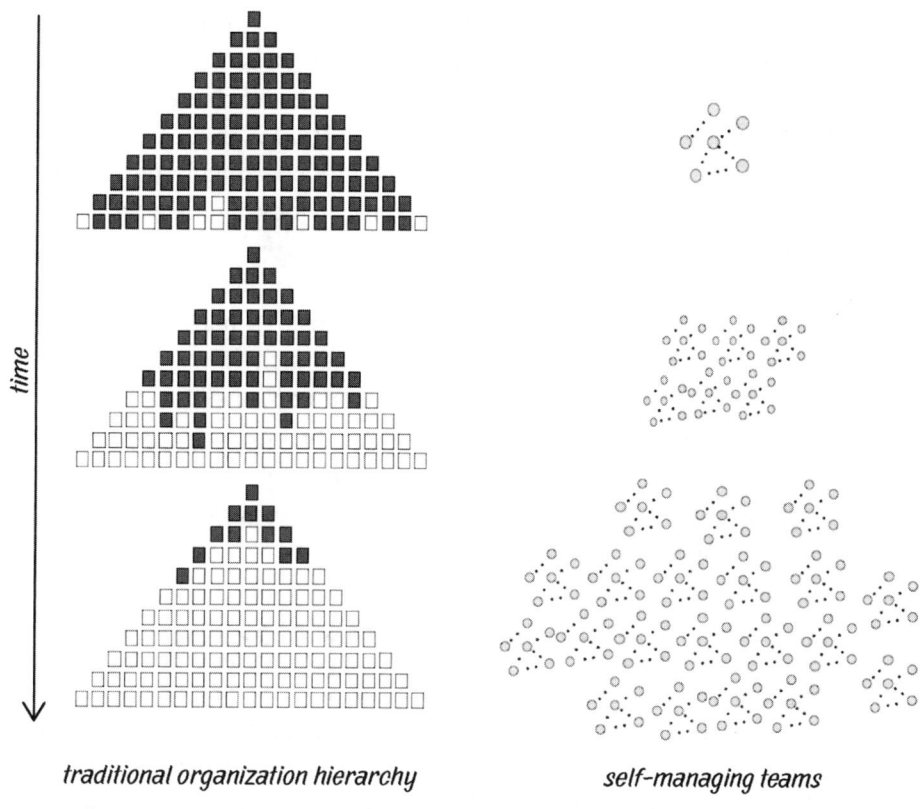

time

traditional organization hierarchy   *self-managing teams*

Figure 7.1 Over time, agile organizations must trim their hierarchy by transferring responsibility and authority to self-managing teams.[2]

At first, outside specialists supporting agile teams can report into a traditional organization hierarchy. In fact, early in the transition, the organization may actually need more specialists to keep agile teams from waiting for help. As agile teams become more self-sufficient, however, the organization will typically not need as many people with specialized skills. In turn, the organization typically will not need as many managers for specialized skill silos.

2. Adapted from www.bbvaopenmind.com/en/articles/the-organization-of-the-future-a-new-model-for-a-faster-moving-world/.

Once an organization has decided to commit to working in an agile way, it must make it clear that the agile teams are at the center of how the organization works and how customer value is created, and that everything else must be in service to those teams. Specialized skill areas that can't be absorbed into cross-functional teams can be converted into coaching/knowledge transfer centers, but the organization must always be looking for ways to help teams to be more self-sufficient.

Examples of skill areas and supporting teams that may still need to exist even after agile teams have become "mainstream" include employment law compliance, security (both physical and cyber), other forms of compliance, contracting, litigation, and compensation, among others. The sorts of skill areas that may need specialized support are those that agile teams need infrequently and that require (sometimes licensed) knowledge that an ordinary team would not invest in obtaining.

GROWING SELF-MANAGING TEAMS ORGANICALLY

Chapter 2 explored how self-managing teams form by helping interested people to self-organize. The discussion there hinted that there was an upper limit to how large these teams could become, usually somewhere around nine people. The reasons for this limit have to do with the complexity of communication networks within the team, which varies depending on the number of people, their level of trust, and the nature of the work on which they are collaborating (see Table 7.1).

Table 7.1 The Complexity of Communication Networks Within Teams Limits Their Size

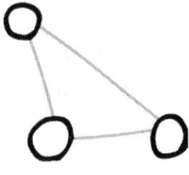

A small team that has just started to build a valuable proposition. There are just enough people to build a minimum viable product.

This team might still be missing a few people with infrequently needed skills, such as marketing, finance, operations, security, and so forth, but they can usually obtain these from other parts of the organization, provided that they don't have to wait for people with these skills to be available to help.

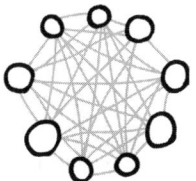

A medium-to large-size team that contains all skills it needs to create valuable outcomes for customers.

While this team is fully capable of serving its current customers, it may still find opportunities for growth by delivering outcomes that expand its customer base.

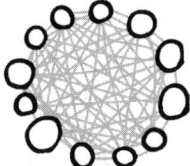

If a team grows too large, its internal communication network can become too complex so that the team is no longer capable of being fast and effective. Some team members will likely have better connections with each other, which can lead to the formation of team subcultures and subgroups that harm team cohesion and communication.

WHAT TO DO WHEN TEAMS BECOME TOO LARGE

When a team grows too large and starts to lose effectiveness, organizations try a number of strategies to break up the teams (see Table 7.2.)

Table 7.2 Strategies for Splitting Teams When They Become Too Large to Be Effective

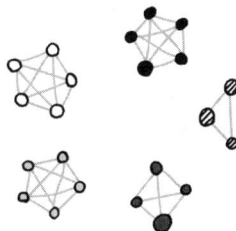

One option to split a team is to organize by components of the overall solution, which are typically assembled by an integration team. For example, for a company like Reliable Energy, these components might each focus on a different functional area of the business. For example:

- Customer billing
- Network maintenance and monitoring
- Power generation
- Customer service

Other organizations, especially those that do not produce physical products, like financial institutions, often organize by skill area. For example:

- Marketing
- Legal

- User experience
- Product development
- Operations
- Security

The advantage of these structures is that the people on each of these teams do similar kinds of work, which can make it easier to collaborate.

The principal disadvantage of these structures is that no one team has any affinity with the customers, and no one team is accountable for delivering value to those customers. Because they need to collaborate with each other to deliver value, they often take a very long time to deliver anything. In addition, because no one is really responsible for value, they typically lack the ability to self-manage to improve their results.

This organizational pattern is the foundation for the organizational silos that create many of the problems that traditional organizations experience.

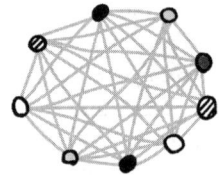

A better alternative is splitting a large team into smaller teams aligned with specific customer outcomes, so that each smaller team has all the people and skills it needs to deliver one or more specific outcomes, from idea to actual customer benefit. This model is sometimes called a *feature team* model, assuming that a feature produces an independent increment of customer value.

This way of splitting up a team is especially effective if dependencies on the other teams can be eliminated, so that each team is able to act independently to improve customer outcomes. For example, an energy organization like Reliable Energy might include teams focused on:

- Providing energy storage
- Enabling customers to buy and sell energy on the open market
- Creating and servicing secure microgrids
- Meeting the charging needs of operators of electric vehicles

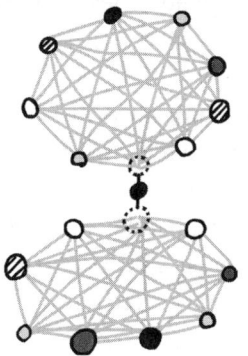

When dependencies cannot be fully eliminated, and multiple teams need to collaborate to deliver a specific customer outcome, the teams must expend extra effort to coordinate their activities.

This example illustrates a situation where one person (e.g., the Product Owner in Scrum) takes the same role for both teams to help them align on goals and outputs so that the work of each team contributes to achieving a greater goal. In this way, optimal clarity and alignment is guaranteed and communication overhead is reduced to a minimum.

SCALE AGILITY BY REMOVING DEPENDENCIES

Many organizations worry about how to scale agility. They can see how a single team can be agile, but their organizations produce products or services that—at least the way they are organized today—require the efforts of many teams. Because they know of no other way, they envision that scaling agility requires adding oversight and coordination mechanisms to synchronize the work of multiple agile teams.

When these organizations add these oversight and coordination functions, they find that the agility that one self-managing team experiences slowly dies as the oversight and coordination become more intrusive. External oversight and coordination kill self-management. As the responsibilities of each team narrow and fragment, they begin to resemble component teams that don't deliver outcomes to real customers and cannot really inspect and adapt based on feedback from real customers. And pretty soon, the "scaled" agile organization looks and works just like the old organization that it was supposed to replace.

External oversight and coordination kill self-management.

If you want to scale agility, you have to eliminate dependencies. These dependencies take several forms:

- *Skill dependencies* occur when an agile team does not have all the skills it needs to deliver a valuable, useful product or service increment. This problem is solved by the practices described in Chapter 6, in which people with scarce specialist skills are available whenever an agile team needs them. Over time, these specialists can work as coaches to help agile team members acquire the skills, if the team feels that they need the skills within the team.

- *Product dependencies* arise when a product or service is too large and complex for a single team to deliver. This problem can be solved by breaking the product or service into smaller products or services, each of which provides unique and valuable outcomes for a smaller group of people, and each of which is delivered by a single team. This practice was described briefly in Chapter 2, with a footnote to a supporting article.

- *Cross-team dependencies* exist when the first two kinds of dependencies cannot be completely eliminated. Dealing with these is beyond the scope of this book, but is covered in another book in this series, *The Nexus Framework for Scaling Scrum: Continuously Delivering an Integrated Product with Multiple Scrum Teams*, published by Addison-Wesley Professional.

Eliminating these dependencies lets agile teams do what they are supposed to do: deliver value incrementally and empirically based on feedback. Bolting on traditional management oversight and coordination practices just complicates the scaling problem.

CONSOLIDATING SUPPORT AND ELIMINATING OPPOSITION

In every change, some people will benefit and thrive, and others will experience loss of influence. The people with the most to lose are the ones who benefited from the old system. If people in this group cannot find a new purpose in the new organization, they are likely to create impediments to the change. These impediments can range from passive nonsupport to explicit and forceful opposition. Even when the benefits for the organization are clear, don't expect that people with something to lose will simply accept the change for the greater good.

EXPECT, EMBRACE, AND ENCOURAGE ATTRITION

As work continues to shift from the traditional organization to agile teams, the traditional organization hollows out. With agile teams taking on more work and increasing their autonomy, the organization needs fewer managers to oversee work. Some of the more experienced employees, initially in line to take up management roles, shift their focus to improvements that will help teams to become even more autonomous, including automated tests, automated deployments, learning resources to share expertise, and related improvements.

Doreen gets most excited when she hears that Nick has decided to participate in a workgroup aimed at increasing coaching skills in the organization. He was the first of her executives to realize the potential opportunity to keep growing in his role in the organization beyond a strict management path. Other leaders saw similar opportunities and took similar steps to grow themselves to find new ways to contribute.

Nick and Doreen have come to realize that the new Reliable Energy will need less management in the future. And apparently, they are not the only ones who have figured this out.

One day, Doreen receives an email from Carl.

Doreen,

Since the acquisition of Energy Bridge, I have seen a number of changes in the organization that I cannot agree with.

By allowing teams to deviate from processes and default reporting structures, there is no way that we are able to make sure that people comply with the rules we created. Since my team have also started adopting agile practices, they are continuously rebelling against the procedures we created to protect them from making mistakes.

Some of my most successful project managers recently left, because:

1. Their responsibilities are now performed by other roles in the agile teams.

2. Your changes in the executive bonus plan have given them less direct influence to achieve their bonus and be successful.

It took me 20 years to make a career at this company and become head of PMO by working hard, challenging people, and being resilient and straight with them. Last week we had a meeting with my colleagues in the PMO and we collectively feel as if all these accomplishments no longer count and that our roles have been hollowed out ever since we acquired Energy Bridge.

To that end, I hereby submit my resignation. I have accepted an opportunity at another company. I will be leaving Reliable Energy at the end of the month.

Regards,

Carl

As more teams embrace and become effective at self-management, the organization will have less need for traditional managers. Astute managers fear this, and their fears are not unfounded. There are other jobs that the organization needs to have done, but if a person wants to be a traditional manager, they will not find those kinds of opportunities in an agile organization; they will need to seek employment elsewhere.

> *As more teams embrace and become effective at self-management, the organization will have less need for traditional managers.*

Carl's email is an example of the growing tension in a part of the organization that gradually discovers that the responsibilities of a traditional manager will change. Like Carl, some people will keep opposing the change. They don't believe in the change, and they're not going to support it.

In the scenario with Carl, Doreen appears to have made a mistake: She did not see the situation coming, and she did not work proactively with Carl to plan a graceful exit. While his departure is unregretted, it might have been handled better to avoid internal tension and conflict.

Some organizations make the mistake of denigrating people who, for whatever reason, chose to disagree with the path the organization is taking. Sometimes their objections are constructive and addressing them can actually improve the overall solution. Frequently, people who defend the old system were the ones who made it, and the organization of the past, successful. Their criticisms often uncover valid points, and professional respect demands that they are able to give voice to their concerns.

Once their concerns are addressed, however, continued opposition undermines the success of the initiative. In these cases, it's best to find a respectful way of parting company. Beyond professional courtesy, there is a practical reason: There will always be people remaining in the organization who respect the departing leader, and they will feel better about staying if they feel that people are treated with respect.

Giving audience to dissenting voices is an important part of establishing an environment of trust and transparency. But once issues are resolved, they need to be left behind.

BE MINDFUL OF LEADERSHIP STYLES, AND ACT ACCORDINGLY

Chapter 5 introduced four different leadership styles: combative, compliant, competitive, and catalytic. The challenge for agile leaders seeking to change their organizations is that they will need to eliminate combative and compliant leadership styles, while helping people with a competitive leadership style to gradually adopt a catalytic leadership style.

As Figure 5.1 suggests, it is very difficult for people with combative and compliant leadership styles to adopt a catalytic leadership style. It's not impossible, but it takes a lot of effort and willingness to let go of a lot of leadership characteristics that a person might feel are the foundations for their past success. Our past experience suggests that people in these two categories, like Carl, usually decide to leave the organization. If they don't leave voluntarily, and they won't change, they need to be helped to move on, up to and including help with outplacement, if they choose to leave the company.

Treating people fairly is one way that agile leaders help to establish a culture of trust and transparency.

People with a competitive style of leadership can evolve their leadership style if they believe that doing so will result in better performance for the organization. What they must let go of is their tendency to view everything as a competition with their peers for status; they must be able to put other people's growth first if they are to grow themselves. This requires a very significant shift in mindset, and many people take a long time to make the transition. These people usually make their own decisions to "compete" somewhere else.

People who have experience as coaches and mentors usually find developing a catalytic leadership style to be very natural, and they are able to grow their capabilities by building on these past experiences. They also tend to find a natural affinity for experiencing a sense of personal and professional satisfaction in seeing others grow and develop.

BUT BEWARE UNWANTED ATTRITION

Change is unsettling, and people react to the stress of change in a variety of ways. When people don't understand how a change might affect them, they can imagine worst-case scenarios that can cause them to want to leave the stressful situation, even if that means finding other employment. Their response is completely reasonable, even if their fears are unfounded. Leaders need to recognize that change is stressful. They need to listen carefully to what people are saying about the change, and pay even more attention to what people are *not* saying.

Leaders need to continually communicate why decisions are being made, how they will measure results, and how they will adapt when they need to change course. People in traditional organizations are accustomed to a lack of transparency, and they will typically not fully trust what leaders say until they see their words backed by actions. Careful listening and observation can help leaders detect when they need to improve communication, increase transparency, and put their words into practice.

It has been our experience as consultants that good people leave organizations because they no longer feel they belong. By helping team members see how they fit in, and can even thrive, leaders can help to prevent the departure of the very people they cannot afford to lose.

SOMETIMES YOUR GREATEST CRITIC CAN BECOME YOUR BIGGEST ALLY

Sometimes, a team member will be skeptical of the change and will seem to always find fault with whatever the organization does. Dealing with this sort of person can be one of the greatest challenges the agile leader will face. No one likes criticism, agile leaders included, but they need to resist the temptation to dismiss the criticism as simply troublemaking. Critics can be right, and they may see something that the agile leader does not.

Agile leaders need to develop the habit of listening to all points of view, not just the ones that support their positions. Sometimes people just want to know that they are being heard, and demonstrating openness to diverse viewpoints helps to promote transparency and build trust. Sometimes the critic has a unique perspective that helps everyone to reach a better decision. It also benefits everyone to develop communication skills that help themselves and teams to bring forth and discuss differing viewpoints, backed by data and not just opinion.

Only after critics have had their opportunity to make their case should agile leaders start to consider whether the goal of the criticism is simply disruption. Some people really do thrive on creating conflict, and empowering them is also a mistake. It's a fine line to walk, and agile leaders need to create open opportunities for discussion without fostering disruption. Constructive criticism is healthy, provided that its aim is to create improvements that can be tested with experiments. But if the will for experimenting is lacking, then the critic's intent is simply to foment conflict—and leaders will need to move swiftly to stymie it.

SILENT SUBVERSION IS WORSE THAN OPEN OPPOSITION

The real problem is not the people who openly oppose the change, but rather the people who appear to go along with the change but always find ways to quietly but subtly resist. They may honestly feel that self-managing teams are a bad practice, or simply anarchy. And if the teams are immature and lack appropriate support and coaching, those skeptics would be correct. Unfortunately, their actions and lack of support create the very conditions that they claim to be concerned about.

As a leader, if you have evidence that mature self-managing teams produce results and enable the kind of responsive, creative employee engagement that your organization needs to be successful, you cannot vacillate in your support for agility or you will kill it.

This means one thing: People in a leadership role in your company must be effective supporters of self-managing teams. Those who are not might need help to understand why they need to support the teams to help the organization succeed. If this persuasive effort fails, they won't have a place in the organization, and they need to go. If they do not reach this conclusion on their own, as Carl has, they need to be helped to this conclusion.

Most people in leadership roles are highly intelligent and, even more so, politically astute. If they understand that their goals and those of the organization no longer align, they will realize they need to move on. It's best for agile leaders to address this issue in direct terms, out of respect for the person's past contributions and future career potential, even if that career may be in another organization. They may need time and assistance to find another role. If they have been top contributors to the organization in the past, they have earned this respect.

The worst thing for a person who doesn't agree with the change is to stay in a place where they no longer want to work. At best, they will be unhappy and unmotivated; at worst, they may sabotage, unwittingly or not, the things the rest of the organization is trying to accomplish. Agile leaders need to actively look for signs that a person truly doesn't want to be part of the change.

In such a case, the person needs to leave, and effective leaders can help these employees move on with their careers in the most effective way possible.

Agile leaders need to actively look for signs that a person truly doesn't want to be part of the change.

Some project managers, like Carl, view comprehensive planning as the mark of a true professional. People who believe that it's possible to gather comprehensive requirements or to create comprehensive plans don't really understand complexity or embrace an empirical approach. Perhaps they don't perceive that a particular problem is complex, or they do not have enough experience working on complex problems to have experienced the failure of traditional plan-based approaches to solving the problem. If they can't be brought around to understand and embrace empiricism, they will be a constant source of conflict for the teams on which they work.

Managers are not the only people who may feel that they don't want to work in a new way. Some traditional product managers liked what they used to do; they like creating comprehensive requirements documents and being the sole point of contact with business stakeholders, and they don't like being part of a cross-functional team. Meanwhile, some developers and other team members want to work alone and not be part of a team. If these people can't adapt, they don't belong on a self-managing team. Agile leaders will have to either find other work for them to do or let them go.

WHAT IF SENIOR EXECUTIVES ARE THE PROBLEM?

This problem often arises in organizations in which the move to agility is primarily led by middle management. Middle managers sometimes endure unfair criticism, which suggests that they are the people who most ardently resist change. In most organizations, middle managers are actually the people with the deepest commitment to the organization, the operational knowledge, and the cultural connections; they keep the organization functioning despite a revolving door at the top of the organization.

When senior executives oppose the change, or perhaps more often, are indifferent to or delegate the change, the agile initiative usually fails to gain enough traction to be successful. Without senior executive support, departmental and specialty skill silos remain intact, crippling agile teams with a matrixed management approach that prevents cross-functional teams from forming and self-managing.

Without executive support, real change will not be sustainable.

In these cases, the only solution is for trusted advisors, usually from within the company, to help senior executives come to the conclusion that the organization will fail unless it changes. Once they understand this, their resistance or indifference usually fades and they provide the support the organization needs. Otherwise, they leave, and someone with greater understanding and commitment takes their place.

REALIGN COMPENSATION PLANS

Traditional organizations typically reward individuals for achieving individual results. Sometimes they will recognize team performance, but even then they often single out individuals on teams for special recognition.

An agile organization recognizes that nearly everything that it achieves is the result of a team's work. Agile leaders need to make a conscious shift away from individual performance rewards and compensation plans, and toward team recognition.

At the same time, individuals compete in the labor market for compensation, and people want to know that their compensation reflects their value in the broader employment market. Different people will have different marketability depending on the value of their skills in the market.

So how do leaders balance the need to reward teams with the need to ensure that individuals feel their compensation reflects their market value? Most organizations are familiar with a base pay plus variable pay compensation system. For an agile organization, the base pay for an employee reflects the market value of their skills, which is influenced by factors such as demonstrated skill proficiency and experience. An employee's variable pay would then be based on team performance, which usually reflects the value to the organization that the team creates by delivering customer outcomes.

Truly self-managing teams should be able to decide how to divide a variable compensation pool amount between team members, although the ability to do so without contention is the mark of a very high-performing team. Leaders may need to help teams to decide by coaching them, so long as they are not perceived by the team as trying to influence the result.

Leaders and staff in "coaching areas" should be measured by how effectively they support teams, with the greatest emphasis given to how effectively they transfer knowledge to agile teams, and how effectively those teams deliver value to their customers. These people in supporting roles can still work in an agile team, supporting the other teams to create value.[3]

REALIGN CAREER PATHS

As mentioned earlier, agile organizations tend to have less hierarchy than traditional organizations. In consequence, agile leaders have fewer opportunities to reward people through promotion to higher levels in the hierarchy. They have to find other ways to provide people with rewarding careers, such as improving their sense of autonomy, mastery, and purpose.

Promotions reward people in two ways: They increase a person's compensation, and they increase a person's prestige in the organization. Compensation was already discussed in the context of rewarding individual performance, and the same approach works for promotion-related salary increases.

Finding alternatives that increase a person's prestige without using promotion requires understanding that much of the increase in prestige that comes with

---

3. For more information on this topic, see this blog: https://evolutionaryleadership.nl/news/all-teams-need-to-be-agile/.

a promotion stems from recognizing the promoted person as having valuable experience and expertise that enable them to have influence beyond their own individual concerns. The most logical expression of this understanding in an agile organization is to recognize people for their ability to grow others by coaching and mentoring. Doing so provides the coach/mentor with public recognition that their experiences are both valuable and valued, without the disadvantages of having to create a new position in the organization's hierarchy.

EMBRACE CATALYTIC LEADERSHIP

As noted in prior sections, and in Chapter 6, leaders in agile organizations need to adopt a catalytic leadership style by gradually evolving their focus from directing to coaching and mentoring. While many leaders have great intuition about helping others to develop, they may benefit from developing their coaching and mentoring skills by being coached and mentored themselves.

Catalytic leaders' goal is to help others develop their ability to recognize opportunities to improve both their own skills and those of their team. They then help those people develop ideas about how they could improve, and support them as they try out those improvement ideas. Effective coaches don't tell others how to improve; they stimulate people to develop their own approaches and improve based on experimentation and feedback.

Catalytic leaders aim to create new leaders.

This means, most importantly, that catalytic leaders are patient. They don't become frustrated when a person's or team's first ideas on how to improve don't produce the hoped-for results. They help people to examine their results for things that they can learn, and encourage them to adapt their approach based on these insights.

Most leaders are on a journey in this respect, and they need to apply the same patience and introspection to their own learning journey. They will not do everything perfectly at once. They may never be perfect. But as long as they are willing to take the time to make thoughtful attempts to learn and improve based on experience, they will get better over time.

REPLACE STATUS MEETINGS WITH TRANSPARENCY

In Carl's last week with Reliable Energy, Doreen gets a call from Maria, head of the power generation business unit.

"Doreen, I've been meaning to call you since I heard that Carl is leaving. I've been watching how the staff on the PMO has gradually been either leaving or moving onto other initiatives, and I've been wondering, without Carl and the PMO, who is going to be running the weekly project status meetings? And who is going to be producing the status reports that Carl used to send out? I use those to keep me informed of what's going on with projects that my business unit is funding."

Doreen replies, "As you know, we've been shifting to a different model for the work the agile teams are doing. Instead of status reports, they've been providing real-time dashboards on their goals for the next release, as well as evidence of their progress toward those goals, including results from customers. I think you've seen that information coming from the Smart Grid teams."

Maria replies, "Yes, their shift toward goals has made it really easy to understand what's going on. It makes a lot more sense to me than the old 'red-yellow-green' status readouts that we used to get."

Doreen replies, "Yes, that's what I've heard from other business unit heads as well. With Carl leaving, we're phasing out the old status reports and moving to real-time goal-based status dashboards."

Maria responds, "Perfect! I was hoping that might be the case. I've heard a lot of complaints about the old reports, and we've all had the experience of a major program reporting 'green' status forever, only to go suddenly 'red' just before something was set to go live."

Doreen replies, "With the phasing out of the old status reports, we accept that plans continuously change, and that the best way to provide visibility into status is for teams to be fully transparent about what they have accomplished and what they are working on. To make that work, we all need to not react to 'bad' news by criticizing teams; that only discourages them from being transparent. Instead, we need to try to help teams overcome their challenges, and to do that we need them to openly share when they are struggling. "

Traditional plan-based status reporting is usually subjective, though sometimes it appears to have a veneer of objectivity when it is based on adherence to schedules, or budgets, or features complete.

As discussed in Chapter 3, everything about a plan-based system is a guess. The features that the organization thinks are needed to achieve the outcomes the organization hopes to produce are a guess, as the budget needed to build those features, and the time that is needed to build those features. Even if a project delivers on time and on budget, it may fail to achieve the hoped-for outcomes.

Traditional status reporting is largely theater. It is the opposite of transparency. Because they are pressured to show positive results, project managers present selective information that casts the work performed, expressed in activities and outputs, in the most positive light possible.

Instead of false reports of progress based on activities and outputs, everyone in the organization needs to understand the goals of the work and the evidence of what the teams have achieved to show progress toward those goals— including, sometimes, evidence that the goals are wrong and need to be reconsidered. The only way to achieve this is to be completely transparent about what the team is working on, and why.

This is a big cultural shift for most organizations. Everyone needs to get comfortable talking about goals and results, rather than activities and outputs. And they need to find ways of sharing this information without creating extra work in the form of status meetings or status reports.

Organizations that are leaving behind traditional approaches also need to become comfortable with partial, incremental results. Sometimes this is a challenge for people: They are used to not having anything useful until the end of a project, at which point they are supposed to get everything. Except they don't get everything, and what they do get is almost always partially wrong.

Instead of expecting to get everything they want at the end, people in the organization need to get comfortable with seeing partial results at regular intervals. When these partial results are aligned with customer outcomes, progress is easy to understand. This is the essence of the agile approach, but many organizations don't understand how much the success of an agile approach depends on transparency.

Transparency can be threatening, however. Stakeholders frequently find out that their understanding of customers' needs was off, and that the "killer feature" that they fought for so fiercely hasn't been used at all by customers. But they can also discover that customers find something else even more valuable than they had understood before, and that knowledge leads to better outcomes for everyone.

Transparency will, at some point, make everyone "look bad." None of us knows as much as we think we do, and if you're going to follow an agile, empirical approach you'll need to accept that you're going to be wrong some of the time. Finding out that you're wrong creates opportunities to learn, but only if your organization's culture is open to that learning.

In fact, when organizations first try to do something new, including embracing agility, they are almost always wrong, because that's when they know the least. Agile leaders must recognize and accept this truth if they are to provide the space and freedom to stimulate teams to learn and improve.

To illustrate this, Ed Catmull describes the way that Pixar turns early "bad" ideas into great movies:

> "Early on, all of our movies suck. That's a blunt assessment, I know, but I choose that phrasing because saying it in a softer way fails to convey how bad the first versions really are. Pixar films are not good at first, and our job is to make them so—to go, as I say, 'from suck to not-suck.' Candor is the key to collaborating effectively. Lack of candor leads to dysfunctional environments."[4]

---

4. Ed Catmull and Amy Wallace, *Creativity, Inc.: Overcoming the Unseen Forces That Stand in the Way of True Inspiration*.

Pixar's "brain trust" process helps establish candor as desirable in this organization. Agile approaches use similar practices like reviews and retrospectives to help teams create the transparency they need to quickly expose bad ideas so that they can improve them into good, or even great, ones.

Agile leaders need to create the space in which teams can learn. They have to demonstrate that everything we think we know could be wrong, and that it's better to find things out as early as possible. And they have to reward teams for being completely transparent.

BE REALISTIC ABOUT HOW LONG THE TRANSITION WILL TAKE, AND WHAT IT MEANS

Descriptions in books like this can sometimes leave the reader with the impression that these transitions are easy, or they will occur quickly. Most organizations actually take many years to reach the point where they can start realigning the organization, and the realignment, in turn, takes many years.

Executives expecting quick results need to reset their expectations. Then again, executives expecting quick results rarely have the patience or the dedication to see through a change like this. They may start the change, but as soon as they can claim some small victory, they will be off to seek some other promotion. Agile change is for the far-sighted and for those willing to put aside their own personal benefit for the betterment of the larger organization.

In fact, self-serving "leaders" don't do well in agile transformations because they cannot see beyond their own self-interest. It's usually the self-serving "leaders" who need to exit the organization for self-managing teams to thrive and for the organization to reap the full benefits of agility. The leaders who thrive in the transition will be those who gain a great sense of satisfaction in helping other people to develop their abilities and to thrive.

REFLECTIONS ON THE JOURNEY

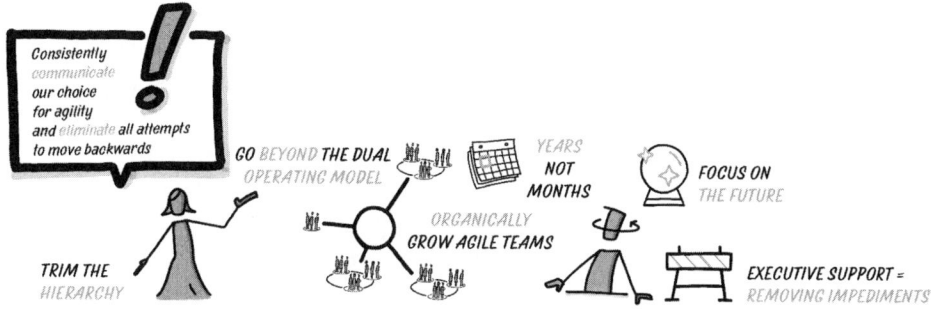

Early in this book, the authors advocated for a *dual operating system* model, in which the nascent agile organization coexists alongside the traditional organization. This is important as the agile organization forms and grows. However, as the new organization grows and matures, the traditional and agile organizations often find themselves in fundamental conflicts on their values and basic ways of working. For example, an organization cannot, in the end, have two different ways of rewarding people: one based on individual accomplishment as determined by management, and the other based on team achievements and team member contributions based on 360-degree feedback.

Eventually, if the agile organization is successful in achieving its goals, it will have earned the right to take on more responsibilities. Agile leadership plays a critical role in gradually transferring more and more responsibilities from the traditional organization to the agile organization. This transfer does not happen all at once, but happens gradually as the agile teams are ready to take on more.

ALIGNING THE CULTURE

Changing the organization's culture is the final and ultimate challenge that all agile leaders face. An organization's culture acts like a gyroscope that keeps it pointed in a consistent direction, even through disruptions and deviations that might otherwise threaten to throw it off course. But this culture gyroscope also works to prevent agile change, and many organizations that fall back during their agile attempts find that their cultural gyroscopes are too strong to change without a tremendous effort. Most organizations simply don't experience enough pain to cause them to need to change quickly and to expend the energy that cultural change requires.

Changing the culture of an organization requires leaders to apply slow, steady, and consistent effort over a very long time. People in the organization need to know that agility is going to work, not only for the organization, but for them personally. They also need to know that it's not just a management fad, and that it will not pass like so many initiatives that have come before. Another catalyst is the realization that the competition never sleeps and is likely also investing in building a more responsive organization. In such cases, it is better to be your own competitor than to get outcompeted.

In the end, to change culture, the people in the organization must embrace agile change as if it was their own idea; the change cannot be something that they feel someone is imposing on them. They must feel that working in an agile way is the most natural way to work, and that working in any other way feels wrong. Once they reach this point, the organization will finally have achieved the agility and resilience that it needs to survive and thrive in a complex world. It will finally be resistant to sliding back to old ways of working.

In many ways, this is nothing new, and it isn't unique to agile change; it is simply human nature. As Lao Tzu is said to have observed more than 6000 years ago:

Leaders are best when people barely know they exist. When their work is done, their aim fulfilled, the people will say, "We did it ourselves."

WHAT MAKES CHANGING CULTURE HARD

It's late on a Friday, after a long week. As she is walking to the car park, Nick calls after Doreen, "Doreen, do you have a moment to chat?"

"Hi, Nick; I was just heading home, but of course. How have you been?"

Nick replies, "I've been well. The agile teams are doing well, mostly. But I keep getting push-back from some of the former managers, and I feel that anytime I turn my attention away from them, they slip back into old habits. I'm beginning to wonder if they are ever going to change. I could use your help."

Doreen responds, "Why do you think they are pushing back? Do they feel that their jobs are threatened? We've tried to make sure that everyone knows that jobs may change, but we value our people and we will work with everyone to find where they can best contribute as long as they are committed to working with us."

Nick says, "I think that's part of it, but not completely. I hear through the grapevine that some people feel lost. Intellectually, they understand they will have work, but they are frustrated that we don't have everything all worked out, yet. I understand their desire for certainty, but I know from my own journey that they just have to relax about that for a while."

Doreen agrees, "I've been through that, too; that tension that comes from fear that things will not work out. Even now, there are days that I wonder what surprises await ahead. But then I look at all the way we have come, and how much better we are at dealing with new challenges, those fears subside and I'm able to refocus."

Doreen continues, "I've heard the same things from other senior leaders. Let's get together, some of us, on Monday to talk about what we can do to help people through the 'valley of despair' that I think all of us have experienced at one time or another."

Almost every person who has been through, or is in the midst of, an organizational transformation says the same thing: Culture is the hardest thing to change. But do they mean when they use the word *culture*? In simple terms, it simply refers to "the way that we do things around here." Culture emerges from the attitudes, values, and goals of people in the organization.

When leaders are trying to change the culture, they are, in effect, pulling the rug out from under the people in the organization. Those people thought they knew what was valued; they thought they knew the right thing to do. Now they are confused. Not long ago, creating detailed plans was the sign of a professional; now it's the sign of someone who is well-meaning but deluded.

Most agile transformations fail because they fail to change the culture.

Some people, like Carl in previous chapters, get angry. Others embrace the change, because they will embrace anything new. Most people internalize the conflict. They superficially go along, but inside they experience tension, and if the change initiative stalls, they are relieved to go back to something they perhaps thought was working fine, even if it wasn't perfect. This is why most agile transformations fail: They fail to change the culture.

Culture can't be directly influenced by people's words or actions. Even the most inspirational leader is only able to influence their organization's culture indirectly. And while rewards affect behaviors and attitudes, which influence culture, leaders cannot "bribe" their employees to embrace new cultural values. Incentives and rewards can backfire spectacularly in the case of agile change when they focus on superficial behaviors rather than on achieving customer-oriented goals.

Culture has its own will and inertia, and it can only be changed slowly, by building trust and changing beliefs and attitudes. Attempts to change the culture are fragile, and even small events can damage the trust that softens attitudes and opens people to new approaches.

AGILE LEADERS MUST FIRST FIND THEIR OWN WAY

The culture that agile leaders need to nurture is focused on two aspects:

- Self-managing teams
- Empiricism

Everything else emerges from these aspects. Anything that fails to support and enhance those two aspects needs to be eliminated.

Once the agile leader has experienced their own internal transformation, and once they have come to understand and embrace the power of empiricism and self-managing teams, their singular task is to help build a bridge between the old culture and the new one for the rest of the organization. The challenges in doing this are summarized in Figure 8.1.

Figure 8.1 Change dynamics when moving toward a new leadership style.[1]

---

1. The pattern is inspired by two books: *The Responsibility Process*, by Christopher Avery, and *Spiral Dynamics*, by Don Edward Beck and Christopher Cowan.

This journey is similar to the one that anyone goes on when they realize that nearly everything about the way they have been working in the past is ineffective, with a focus on how leaders experience the change. The discussion in Chapter 5 touched on these changes, but here the focus is on the transition between the competitive and catalytic leadership styles.

Before the organization starts to shift toward an agile way of working, when it is in a stable condition, leaders typically find that a competitive leadership style is most effective. As the organization starts to shift toward agile ways of working, and especially as leaders need to help teams to self-organize and self-manage, they find that this competitive leadership style is no longer effective.

For a time, leaders may try to deny that this is true, but they will feel a tension between their own personal needs and the needs of the teams. As this tension builds, their internal conflict grows, especially when they find themselves saying one thing, such as "Agile, self-managing teams are our future," and doing things that are in direct conflict with these statements, such as focusing on their own self-interest instead of that of their teams.

For agile leaders to resolve this conflict, their obligations to help the organization and their teams must gradually overrule their own self-interest. For this to happen, agile leaders need to develop a greater sense of personal satisfaction from helping others than they do from advancing their own interests. Or, considering this another way, they must internalize a value system in which their own interests are best served by helping others to grow and achieve more.

BUILD BRIDGES TO THE NEW CULTURE

Once leaders have gone through all these stages, it is their job to help everyone else move forward. A great leader is also capable of helping people out of the tension area as soon as possible, so they can once again achieve stability. And there is a bonus in this for agile leaders: Once the rest of the organization has "crossed the bridge," the agile leaders can focus on helping it to achieve greater things with its newly developed agility (see Figure 8.2).

Figure 8.2 Agile leaders build bridges to help others to embrace new cultural values.

Agile leaders help to build these bridges for others in the organization in several ways:

- They embody and exhibit the new norms that they want the organization to embrace.
- They create psychological safety for others to embrace these new norms without fear of making mistakes.
- They recognize people who embrace the new norms and, most importantly, reward teams who deliver valuable outcomes to customers.

This is not as complex as it might sound. The most important bridge-building behavior is to give people in the organization permission to make mistakes and learn from them. The agile leader must eliminate fear of criticism. This is where empiricism comes in: Transparency, inspection, and adaptation help people to fail fast and learn quickly. The leader will build a bridge as soon as people apply these principles, based on the trust they feel from their leader.

In a complex world, everyone—including leaders—needs to make mistakes to learn from them. As soon as leaders show that they are using empirical principles to learn and improve, teams will start to feel safe enough to do the same.

DON'T CRITICIZE THE PAST, JUST MOVE AHEAD

It's easy to criticize the past, but it's a trap. The problem with criticizing the way the organization worked in the past is that in doing so, you also criticize the people who worked that way. When you do this, people feel shame, and this shame prevents them from moving forward. They feel, "I thought I was doing the right thing, but now it turns out that I was wrong. I'm going to avoid trying anything new until I know that I won't get criticized in the future."

While examining the past is often a good way to improve, in this case it can prevent the organization from moving ahead. The following analogy describes how the organization can simply move ahead:

Imagine that the organization is a person on a journey. In the past, moving on land, walking and running were the best ways to move ahead.

Now imagine that this person has come to the edge of a great ocean. Walking and running won't help the them move ahead; they need to use different strategies, such as swimming. They may also need to learn how to build boats, then learn how to paddle or sail them, to move ahead. It wasn't that their modes of transportation were wrong; they just face different challenges now.

BUILD PSYCHOLOGICAL SAFETY THROUGH RADICAL TRANSPARENCY

The greatest test that catalytic leaders face is how they handle bad news. Combative leaders forcibly suppress any news that does not affirm the direction they have set and crave more control to avoid more unpleasant news. Compliant leaders also seek to reinforce the status quo; they ignore or bury news that does not fit the conventional narrative and install new rules to avoid repetition of that event. Competitive leaders use bad news to blame someone else and demand themselves and others to show more effort to avoid its repetition.

For catalytic leaders, "bad news" simply does not exist. For them, every piece of information is something that can help the organization improve. In consequence, they don't let themselves or the organization get trapped into thinking that information will "make someone look bad." Whereas combative and competitive leaders tend to weaponize information, catalytic leaders use it to make everyone's performance better. The key to doing this is to look at every decision as an experiment that is validated or rejected based on data. Rather than making decisions based on assumptions that may turn out to be false, the catalytic leader helps their organization make assumptions explicit by turning the decision into an experiment.

For example, instead of making planning predictions about progress and then having to "control damage" when those predictions fail, a catalytic leader will frame the plan as an experiment, saying, in effect, "We believe that if we do X, we will see Y improve." If that experiment does not produce the desired results, the leader tries to understand why and supports new experiments as part of the quest to continually improve.

People experiment all the time—they just don't make the experiments explicit. They make assumptions and then they make excuses about why the desired result didn't appear. This attitude, and the blaming and excuse-making that it promotes, prevent people from learning. Moreover, it holds organizations back from achieving their full potential. That is why catalytic leaders do not blame people for "bad news," but rather create the psychological safety to run experiments.

Catalytic leaders make assumptions explicit by creating the psychological safety to run experiments.

By doing this, catalytic leaders signal that information is value-neutral; it is neither positive nor negative. Information needs to be broadly shared because no one can predict who will find that information useful, or who might see something in it that others don't.

Catalytic leaders create psychological safety by:

- Never holding something someone shares against them.
- Respecting privacy, when someone shares something in confidence, and respecting group decisions about sharing unless everyone agrees.
- Taking direct action when anyone does not respect the prior two points.

Only when everyone in an organization feels comfortable about openly sharing observations and information will that organization be able to be responsive to new threats and opportunities.

Build Trust Even While Making Difficult Decisions

Difficult decisions are another test for the catalytic leader. Consider the case where a manager has to implement painful budget cuts including, possibly, having to let some people go. Here's how most organizations deal with a situation like this:

- The combative leader will make a quick decision and get rid of those people who are least obedient to the leader's will.
- The compliant leader will keep those people who have served longest and get rid of those who came in last or were least likely to comply.
- The competitive leader will let the lowest-performing individuals go.

What is the catalytic leader to do? What the authors have done in our own organizations and with our clients is to involve the people who will be affected by the budget cuts and ask them if they can help solve the problem. Although a loss of people may still be unavoidable, this way of approaching the situation has many times led to:

- Increased trust, because people feel involved in the problem.
- Better solutions, because people came up with other, better ideas to cut expenses.

- People volunteering to leave, because they already had intentions to move elsewhere or retire.
- Greater group cohesiveness, because this process involves people in serious decisions that affect their lives.

Teams can even find a way to increase revenues or reduce costs that don't require the organization to let people go, such as taking a pay cut. If the people decide to take a pay cut, however, catalytic leaders should lead by example: They should be the first to volunteer to take a pay cut, if they really believe in the company's future.

SHARE SUCCESS BUT TAKE THE BLAME WHEN NECESSARY

Combative and competitive leaders tend to take credit when things go well, and blame other people when things go wrong. Compliant leaders tend to view the overall system as being the force behind success, and view noncompliance as the reason why things don't go according to plan.

When things go well, catalytic leaders give credit to the people doing the work itself, the team members who are closest to customers. They realize that when teams are performing well, they need to feel that their good results are recognized. Catalytic leaders also realize that without those self-managing teams, nothing in the organization will get done.

At the same time, catalytic leaders reserve the blame for themselves when things are not going well. They realize that helping teams to perform at their peak is the responsibility of the catalytic leader. So, when things are not going well, it is usually because of some shortcoming in their leadership and support.

When teams see that their leaders support them and give them the tools and the freedom to do their best, they feel motivated to improve and reward the support that their leaders are giving them. They recognize the personal commitment that catalytic leadership requires, and they feel an increased sense of obligation to recognize and reward that level of commitment.

ANTICIPATE AND OVERCOME SETBACKS

Unfortunately, an organization's journey to a new culture is almost never easy or smooth. Changing culture is slow and can be painful; it causes people to confront their most deeply held assumptions about how the organization works, and this can cause conflict. Not everyone will want to change, as shown in the case study. Not everyone will see the world in the same way. As a result, people can get stuck or even fall back.

To overcome this, catalytic leaders must show patience and resolve in supporting the change. Their insistence on radical transparency cannot falter. Their singular focus on improving customer outcomes cannot wane. If they care only about business results (making money), the people in the organization will never internalize the cultural shift and their commitment to strive toward better outcomes will be only superficial. For the culture to change, everyone in the organization needs to embrace and embody customer empathy and the pursuit of better results through empiricism.

EVERY ORGANIZATION CARRIES BAGGAGE; MOVING AHEAD MEANS LEAVING IT BEHIND

Nick decides to drop in on one of the teams' meetings. They are discussing the results they got from customers after their most recent releases. He is a little late in arriving, and as he quietly settles in, he senses the energy in the conversation drop.

"Don't mind me; I'm just interested in what you've been learning," Nick interjects.

The team members share skeptical looks, but the conversation picks up, albeit a little awkwardly. The discussion centers on a new set of features that the team delivered. The features were very important to an internal stakeholder, but they don't seem to have been used much, despite a few major customers requesting it. But no one seems to really want to talk about this, at least in front of Nick.

Nick senses this, and searches for some way to cut the ice.

"That's a really interesting finding, and not what we thought we would see. What is your take on what's going on?"

The team looks a little confused. In the past, Nick had a reputation for berating teams when their plans did not produce the intended result. This "new" Nick is not what they were expecting. Finally, one team member speaks up.

"We're not sure. It could be that the users can't find the features and we need to make them more visible. But the data shows that many users tried the feature once and then did not use it again. We think we need to understand their real needs better, to understand what they are really wanting to achieve with these features. Or maybe their needs have changed."

Nick smiles. "That's a really important insight. Sometimes we just have to build something and get it into customers' hands to better understand what they really need. So what sort of experiments are you thinking you might run next, to better understand their needs?"

The atmosphere in the room relaxes, and the conversation continues. And both Nick and the team have learned an important lesson: People can change, and when they do, everyone needs to accept it and move on.

As a leader grows their catalytic leadership skills, it can take time for others in the organization to trust that they have really changed. Teams will tend to expect that compliant leaders will still seek obedience to established direction, or that competitive leaders are simply pretending to behave in a catalytic way while they seek some advantage. It is natural for these teams to not trust their leaders' motives. Leaders transitioning to a catalytic leadership style will need to acknowledge this hesitancy to trust and demonstrate that their ways have changed.

At the same time, leaders who have not shown trust or transparency in the past need to be aware that teams will not suddenly open up just because the leader says they have changed; it takes time and overt demonstrations of willingness to accept transparency for the teams to really start changing. The case study shows this as a simple act, but the reality is more nuanced: It usually takes a long time to build trust, and to do so leaders need to continually demonstrate that their behaviors have changed so that teams will, in turn, be open to changing their own behaviors.

RECOGNIZE THAT HIGH-PERFORMING TEAMS ARE FRAGILE, AND PROTECT THEM

High-performing teams are not, in a sense, natural. They are rare, the result of a unique group of people coming together to create a team that is more capable than the sum of its members' abilities. They are also fragile: Losing or adding team members requires the team to go through the team-forming phase all over again. And since they are fragile, they are worth protecting and nurturing.

When they do need to add members, potentially because one or more members have left, catalytic leaders need to follow the example shared in Chapter 2: They need to let the teams recruit their own members. This does not enable the team to totally avoid having to go through team formation again, but it does create a sense of ownership among existing team members for the success of the re-forming team.

Leaders can support this process when interviewing candidates by focusing on the long-term cross-team cultural fit of a candidate—but only after the team has made their decision on a candidate. If the leader does not feel there is a good fit, the leader should discuss it with the team and decide how to make the decision.

Over time, even the highest-performing teams can stagnate. Having team members leave and bringing on new team members can bring new ideas to a team, and can counterbalance the time and cost of having to re-form the team so long as it is not something the team undertakes frequently.

EVEN THE BEST TEAMS LOSE THEIR FOCUS, SOMETIMES

Just as high-performing sports teams can find it challenging to sustain their performance at a very high level, self-managing teams will likely have their own ups and downs in performance. Catalytic leaders recognize this and help teams to refocus.

Sometimes this takes the form of giving the team members space to step back when the team has been pushing them too hard. This can occur when a team pushes too hard in one direction and members become frustrated when they don't obtain the results they are seeking. When this happens, tensions between team members can grow to the point where the team's cohesiveness suffers.

In other cases, a team may simply have been working too hard to improve their performance while seeing diminishing returns for their efforts. From an outsider's perspective, their performance may be quite high, but their own high standards prevent them from seeing their results in more objective terms.

In both cases, the catalytic leader needs to help the team see their accomplishments in a more realistic light. If they don't, team cohesion may be damaged and team members may slide back to old ways of working. Sometimes this tension is a signal that the team needs to re-form itself and swap out some team members for new members.

USE "SELF-SUSTENANCE" AS A MEASURE OF SUCCESS

> Several years have passed since Reliable Energy embarked on its own agile journey with the acquisition of Energy Bridge. Doreen has stepped away from the day-to-day management of the company and has taken on the role of executive chairperson. This has allowed her to spend more time on cross-industry initiatives, as well as supporting a women-in-technology initiative by coaching emerging leaders on the things Doreen has learned on her own leadership journey.
>
> One Saturday morning, she needs to go into the office to pick up her sketch notebooks, which describe her experiences in learning a new way of leadership. She plans to use some of the pictures that she and Nagesh created in a workshop she is developing for a leadership retreat.
>
> As she nears the office, Doreen stops at a nearby coffee shop. While she is waiting in line, she overhears two young professionals talking about the new jobs they have just started. As she listens, she cannot help but hear that they have both joined teams at Reliable Energy, and she listens more attentively.

The young woman, Jelena, comments, "In my previous job, I was in product management working for a company that produces solar cells. I knew a lot about the technology from my engineering degree, but I didn't have much exposure to real customers. I had never worked on an agile team before, either. And while I'm still learning how best to contribute to the team, I'm really loving the customer interactions and collaborating with my team members."

The young man, Derek, shares similar insights. "I used to work as a developer at a large financial institution. Our team roles were pretty rigid, and we'd hand over our work to operations when we were done with it. I never had much contact with the people actually using what we had built. What I love most about my new team is that we work together to do whatever needs to be done. If someone hasn't done something before, more experienced team members help them. I feel like I've learned more in the last month than I had in several years at my old company. Even more important, although I'm less experienced, my senior team members seem to appreciate me more than anyone ever has at my previous job."

Doreen is tempted to introduce herself and ask them more questions, but she doesn't want them to feel awkward about being overheard. Mostly, she feels a great sense of satisfaction to realize that these two people, whom she has never met before, seem to be embodying the values and principles that she and Nagesh and Nick, and countless others, had worked so hard to get the organization to embrace.

SUCCESS: WHEN THE NEW HAS BECOME THE DEFAULT

When an agile leader is mired deep in the challenges of helping their organization to learn a new way of doing things, success can seem impossibly far off. Such a leader can take comfort in the progress of individual teams and in the professional growth of individuals, but measuring a cultural transformation is often difficult or impossible to achieve.

Success takes many different forms. At the simplest level, becoming an agile organization means that the organization is able to respond quickly and effectively to external threats and new opportunities. How quick is "quick enough" will vary from organization to organization, and from industry to industry.

But many organizations that seem to have achieved agility ultimately slide back to their old ways of working because their underlying cultures did not change. A powerful and charismatic leader might have been able to achieve temporary change, but as soon as that leader retires or moves on to something else, the organization reverts to its prior state.

Real success in changing an organization is achieved only when the change becomes self-perpetuating. When the people in the organization regard the "new" way of working as "simply the way we do things around here." When changing leaders and team members no longer threatens to undermine the progress that the organization has made thus far.

> *Real success in changing an organization is achieved only when the change becomes self-perpetuating.*

In this scenario, Doreen is justified in feeling a sense of accomplishment. While her organization's journey is not over, the change that the organization's leaders set out to achieve has been largely accomplished. It is now self-sustaining, to a large degree.

PLAN FOR SUCCESSION

In addition to helping teams to grow and achieve their full potential, catalytic leaders help others in their organization to become catalytic leaders. No organization can rely on just one leader to change, and in agile organizations there really is no room for combative, compliant, or competitive leaders. For catalytic leaders to succeed, they need to help others to grow their agile leadership skills.

This may feel scary to leaders who wonder, "What do I then do? Will the organization still need me if there are others who are collectively better at what I can do?"

In the authors' experience, an organization can never have too many catalytic leaders. Organizations never really reach a point where they have too many high-performing teams. There will always be teams that need help, people who need coaching, obstacles that need removing, and opportunities that require the organization to adapt and improve in new ways.

Having other people who could step in to do what you do is actually liberating. It allows you to take advantage of new opportunities and challenges, rather than stagnating, doing the same thing, year after year. And having the space to develop new abilities is actually the best way to prevent your own obsolescence.

AGILE JOURNEYS NEVER REALLY END

"Transformation" is really an inapt metaphor for adopting an agile approach. It paints a picture in which the organization starts in one state, the traditional, then through a herculean effort it reaches a new state, where it continues on with relatively little effort.

The reality of agile change is more like preparing for a sporting event like a World Cup football final match. The traditional organization starts in a condition of poor health, just barely able to perform routine activities. Through dedicated improvement and a lot of hard work, it reaches a high level of performance where team members are able to work together to achieve great outcomes and win against their competitors.

But those competitors are getting better all the time. If the organization wants to continue to win, it cannot slip back into its old wasteful ways; it must continually look for new ways to improve. And it must fight against the natural tendency to start letting things slide.

The struggle is never really over, but it does shift when an organization has achieved an agile culture. In traditional organizations, there is always a tension between the group and individuals, and there are always incentives to game the system for personal gain. In an organization with an agile culture, attempts to game the system or to pursue personal gains over team achievements receive swift and strong reactions from the agile value system.

These changes allow the agile leader to do something new: to no longer have to focus on reacting to threats, to be able to focus on finding great people and helping them learn to work in a new way, and to help the organization seek out greater goals, even under challenging conditions of uncertainty. Frameworks like Holacracy[2] and Sociocracy 3.0[3] are designed to keep adapting the organization toward complexity. We have seen numerous clients reach the same level of agility that Doreen has, and we are seeing an increased number of our clients experiment with them.

LOOKING BACK AT THE AGILE LEADER'S JOURNEY

As mentioned in the Introduction, this story is a fictionalized amalgamation of the experiences of the authors, our clients, and our peers. Many organizations rightfully approach their agile implementation in a similar way that Doreen and Nagesh have done in the case study. And since every organization is different, each will need its own failures and opportunities to learn and discover its path toward more agile leadership. While being aware of this, there is one step in the process that is often addressed too late: "Start with culture."

Many of our clients discovered the importance of measuring and designing culture in an agile transformation far too late. Starting with culture and leadership styles first can save you from a lot of frustration, an excessively high cost of change, and wrong expectations.

That is why, in our current approach as consultants, we start with measuring the current culture and predict the possible obstacles beforehand. In this way, the possible obstacles that Doreen encountered in the case study are known upfront and can be taken into account.

---

2. For more information on Holacracy, see www.holacracy.org/ or the book *Holacracy*, by Brian Robertson.
3. For more information on Sociocracy, see https://sociocracy30.org/ or the book *Sociocratie 3.0*, by Jef Cumps.

After reading this book. leaders will ideally be more aware of the cultural implications and corresponding leadership challenges it surfaces. This final chapter ends with a summarized guideline on how to approach an agile leadership transformation. The approach is similar to the one Doreen took, with the exception that culture focus and leadership style awareness have moved forward.

Here's the approach that has worked best for us and our clients:

1. *Choose a complex problem*. The best way to start experimenting with agile teams is in the environment that needs it most due the complex nature of the work.
2. *Create a cell*. Creating an "agile cell" creates a safe space that is focused on fast learning without having to worry or disrupt the current organization structures and culture.
3. *Start with culture*. Understanding and designing culture from the beginning, using the leadership styles from Chapter 5, is crucial and can save you a lot of frustration.
4. *Invite participants*. Invite people from the traditional organization to volunteer to participate in the agile initiative and select the right people with the right leadership skills and culture.
5. *Refresh your leadership*. Add new hires with fresh insight to this group of leaders.
6. *Create a great vision*. With this group of leaders, create a compelling vision and mission.
7. *Involve the teams*. Let teams self-select around this vision and mission.
8. *Have trust and patience*. Implementing agility and changing toward a catalytic leadership style is hard and requires patience and trust.

REFLECTIONS ON THE JOURNEY

SELF-MANAGING TEAMS

EMPIRICISM

LEADERS GO FIRST

FUTURE FOCUS

PEOPLE CAN CHANGE

IT'S A JOURNEY: **WE ARE NEVER EVER REALLY DONE...**

This book saved cultural change for the end, both because it's the hardest thing to change, and because changing the culture requires doing well all the other things described so far: growing high-performing cross-functional teams, protecting them from harm, removing impediments, and gradually deconstructing the hierarchy. In fact, just by doing these things, you will change the culture, so that cultural change actually happens all along.

The more important realization for organizations should be that the "agile transformation" is never really done. Some leaders think that change means going from one steady state (the traditional organization) to a new steady state (the agile organization), and that once this state is achieved, things will quiet down. It's a mistake to expect this kind of settled contentment, and here's why: The new, agile organization will need to continually respond to new threats and opportunities. The conditions that drove the organization toward agility will never just go away, so the organization and its teams will have to continually adapt to those changes.

In the end, agility is not really a state of being as much as it is a way of continually learning and adapting. But there is some good news: The act of adopting an agile way of working prepares teams and their organizations to make this change. Instead of optimizing a static process, they learn to optimize their adaptability. And adaptability, in today's complex and sometimes chaotic world, is what enables organizations to thrive and grow, even while everything around them is changing.

PATTERNS AND ANTI-PATTERNS FOR EFFECTIVE LEADERSHIP

Table A.1 describes traditional leadership behaviors that are less effective in helping teams to develop effective self-managing behaviors, alongside behaviors that agile leaders can adopt to help their teams develop effective self-managing behaviors. It provides a quick reference to which agile leaders can refer to help to catch themselves from falling back into old habits.

Table A.1 Traditional leadership behaviors that can hamper agility, and their agile counterparts

Less Effective	More Effective
As a leader, I should bear all responsibilities.	As a leader, I'm responsible for helping individuals and teams to grow and take responsibility.
Decisions need to be taken by one single authority and then be cascaded down to those who do the work.	Decisions need to be taken by those who do the work using direct feedback from customers. Authority is everywhere.
My power in the organizations is determined by my ability to have influence on others.	My power in the organization is determined by my ability to enable others to take responsibility.
Not knowing something is a weakness, so we need to make sure we know everything before we act.	Not knowing something is a fact of life, so I need to institutionalize transparency and continuous learning.

Less Effective	More Effective
I need to be the most talented individual.	I need to make sure teams are more talented than any individual.
I need to keep people as busy as possible to make sure we utilize our resources in the most efficient way.	I need to provide people with a goal, so they can use their knowledge to focus on accomplishing the greatest results.
People need to comply with the rules, so we are in control.	People need to continuously reshape the rules, so we can deal with change.
Winning means to be visible and on stage.	Winning means to work in the shadows and enable others to take the stage.
When faced with an impossible challenge, people need to be motivated.	People are intrinsically motivated, so when challenged they need personal guidance.
Successful change is determined by setting a goal and motivating people around that goal.	Successful change is determined by having the right people and involving them in creating a greater goal.
I need to protect my people from making mistakes.	I need to create a safe environment where people learn from their mistakes.

DOREEN'S SKETCHNOTES

This appendix collects the sketchnote summaries presented at the end of each chapter to provide a quick visual reference for the book as a whole.

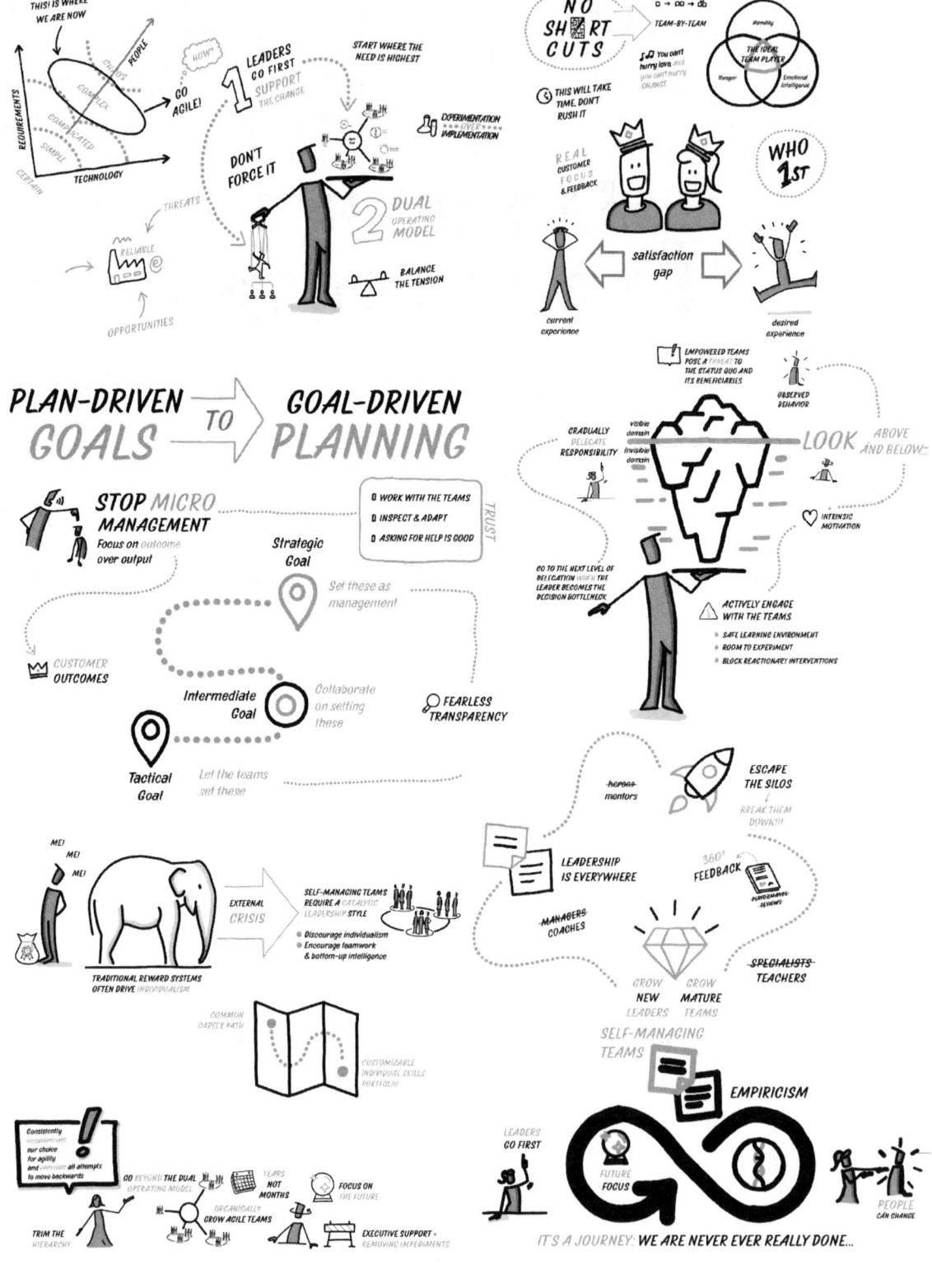

INDEX

Photo by izusek/gettyimage

Register Your Product at informit.com/register

Access additional benefits and **save 35%** on your next purchase

- Automatically receive a coupon for 35% off your next purchase, valid for 30 days. Look for your code in your InformIT cart or the Manage Codes section of your account page.

- Download available product updates.

- Access bonus material if available.*

- Check the box to hear from us and receive exclusive offers on new editions and related products.

Registration benefits vary by product. Benefits will be listed on your account page under Registered Products.

InformIT.com—The Trusted Technology Learning Source

InformIT is the online home of information technology brands at Pearson, the world's foremost education company. At InformIT.com, you can:

- Shop our books, eBooks, software, and video training
- Take advantage of our special offers and promotions (informit.com/promotions)
- Sign up for special offers and content newsletter (informit.com/newsletters)
- Access thousands of free chapters and video lessons

Connect with InformIT—Visit informit.com/community

the trusted technology learning source

Addison-Wesley • Adobe Press • Cisco Press • Microsoft Press • Pearson IT Certification • Que • Sams • Peachpit Press

 Pearson